# CLOSELY OBSERVED TRAINS

# CLOSELY OBSERVED TRAINS

## A nostalgic look back at a decade of change on Britain's railways

## John Stretton

SLP

Silver Link Publishing Ltd

First published in January 1994

British Library Cataloguing in Publication Data

A catalogue record for this book is available from the British Library

ISBN 1 85794 019 9

Except where credited otherwise, photographs are by the author.

Silver Link Publishing Ltd
Unit 5
Home Farm Close
Church Street
Wadenhoe
Peterborough  PE8 5TE
Tel/fax  (0832) 720440

Printed and bound in Great Britain

**6 January 1982**
Twilight of the Gods? Whilst the 'Deltics' had all that attention on the East Coast, a '50' quietly going about its business, nicely captured in the evening lights of Exeter St Davids (as are the delightful period wooden awnings). No 50011 *Centurion* waits for the road to run to Laira with empty stock. *Colin Marsden*

# CONTENTS

*22 April 1983*
Closely observed, but unusually; and who said there is no devotion to diesels? Hushed surroundings accompany a reverent fan 'worshipping' No 47422 as it stands between duties at Liverpool Street station.

# INTRODUCTION

In 1981 Hugh Ramsey, who was producing the early issues of the excellent and long-lamented *Railway Reflections* magazine, commented during one of our conversations that by and large we enthusiasts had not taken as many photographs of the railways of Britain 20 years or so earlier as we should have done, as the daily scene had seemed so permanent and thus we had taken it for granted. He added that perhaps we should now make a conscious effort to record the everyday scene around us, as things were still changing. How wise he was.

For my part, I wish I had had more foresight as I sat by the lineside at Thurmaston, four miles north of Leicester, in the late 'fifties/early 'sixties. I took the odd shot of 'Jubilees' and later 'Scots' and 'Britannias' on express work, but seeing them every day, especially working such trains as the 'Thames-Clyde Express' on my way home from school, they were nothing unusual. Spotting trips to 'foreign' parts warranted the camera, but I still lacked the foresight to capture a wide range of subjects, even when the sun shone. In part this was down to having much more primitive equipment at that time and each film only having 12 exposures, but another problem was trying to finance my hobby from the modest resources of a schoolboy's pocket-money!

Fortunately, Hugh's prophetic words did not fall on stony ground, and I resolved not to repeat the omissions of earlier years. Armed with much better equipment - and fairly quickly a camera each for black and white and colour - and films with faster emulsion speeds, leading to much greater flexibility in poorer lighting conditions, I began recording the contemporary railway scene in the certain knowledge that, with the passage of time, much of what I was photographing would disappear. What I could not have anticipated at the time, however, was the sheer scale of the changes that were to unfold during the 1980s.

I would argue that the years 1980-89 saw more change throughout our railway system than any other previous decade. Future historians of Britain's railways will, I believe, view the radical developments of the decade as more significant than other great milestones, such as the Grouping of 1923, Nationalisation in 1948, the Modernisation Plans of the mid-'fifties, Beeching, or even the end of steam in 1968. Virtually every facet of our railway system is now in a different shape from that of 1980 and I have tried in this book to depict aspects of that change, largely using a medium for which I feel the railway scene has always been so suited - black and white photography.

As an illustration, in April 1983 my wife Judith was travelling to a holiday by train from Watford. Whilst seeing her off I idly photographed the suburban platforms at Junction station, not expending a lot of effort as neither the architecture nor the ageing EMUs particularly interested me; but within weeks those platforms were stripped of their buildings in the course of a redevelopment scheme, and within a couple of years those same '501' EMU sets, so long a part of the North London railway landscape, were consigned to the scrapheap. The process of change that was to be the hallmark of the decade was gathering momentum and that pace has seen me struggling to keep abreast of it ever since.

Looking back, the scene was set at the dawn of the decade with the demise of the 'Deltics'. It had seemed like only yesterday that these diesel giants had displaced Gresley's magnificent 'A4s' from the East Coast Main Line; could it really have been twenty years since I had savoured the sight of No 60024 *Kingfisher* racing down the bank at Essendine in the last year of steam haulage of the non-stop 'Elizabethan'? Now the 'Deltics' were in their turn to be replaced. I missed seeing most in their last days, but I still savour the memory of No 55016 *Gordon Highlander* powering its way westwards out of Slough, in the sunshine of 28 November 1981 on one of its farewell tours. Whether my two small children appreciated the wait in the cold wind, however (this, like many tours, was running late), is another matter!

The prolonged wake for the 'Deltics' in their final days was a foretaste of what was to come, and should have given us some warning for the future. As the final four engines were withdrawn from service in January 1982, there were many who raised eyebrows at this manifestation of so much affection lavished on a form of traction lacking the obvious aesthetic appeal of a steam locomotive, and one which had been so often dismissed as 'boxes on wheels'. Before the end of the 'eighties, however, there would be other, perhaps more surprising, subjects.

Class '40s' - 'Whistlers' - soon attracted their own brand of followers. As numbers declined, the remaining engines garnered attention in inverse proportion to their diminishing stock and much interest soon focused on the pioneer loco, the former D200. Offered to and declined by the National Railway Museum, it had been languishing out of use at Carlisle Kingmoor, somewhat ignominiously as No 40122, when enthusiasts, some in BR's employ, determined to save it. Repaired and repainted in its original green livery it returned, phoenix-like, to duties and truly became a celebrity. Finally withdrawn in May 1988, it had survived the last of its sisters by a good two years and was then graciously accepted as a valued exhibit by that same NRM!

This set a pattern for other celebrity repaints through the decade. No 37350, actually the Class leader, regressed to its original colour scheme and number D6700, and No 50050 reverted to D400, turned out by Laira in near-original blue livery paid for by the readers of *Rail* magazine. But probably the most charismatic of transformations was that of No 25322. Ignominiously, in this guise it was withdrawn in February 1984, to be re-instated just three months later, lovingly and superbly restored by apprentices at Tyseley as D7672 and named by them *Tamworth Castle*. Resplendent in two-tone green, BR put it back to work and it survived until the end of the decade, latterly becoming much sought after for special train duties.

But the repainting of individual locomotives was just one aspect of a much more enlightened approach to liveries in general that developed during the 'eighties. The 'seventies had stagnated, locos looking ever more drab and anonymous under an all-pervading blanket of Corporate Blue. Coaching stock wore a boring uniformity of blue and grey; and stations, publicity and stationery received seemingly no attention at all. Into the 'eighties, all this changed as fragmented and increasingly mercurial livery policy decisions eventually brought recognition that variety actually appealed to the public and led to whole Regions and Sectors receiving their own colours.

Inter-City was soon into the process, with a kaleidoscope of variations on a basic theme; Railfreight, fairly new as an identifiable independent unit, had two new livery launches in a short space of time; and Provincial/Regional Railways, Parcels, Departmental, Research, and even sub-divisions within these, all strove to make their own statement. There were attempts at controlling the proliferation, but once Pandora's box had been opened, there was no going back. This newfound freedom even extended down to depot level, with the likes of Stratford, Tinsley and Thornaby intent on putting their own stamp on whatever they operated. And, as if that were not enough, there was yet more variety associated with the various anniversaries that occurred during the decade, such as GW150.

Then there were other events worth recalling. There has always been change and rationalisation within the system from the earliest days - lines, stations and services opened and closed - but during the decade we had the spectacle of BR being forced to back down on two significant closure proposals.

The former Midland main line from Leeds to Carlisle, via Settle Junction and Appleby, is now a much celebrated route, but it is only through the determined

**1 March 1987**
Once a common sight - at least externally - signal boxes were swept away in the 1980s with little ceremony and in great numbers. One such was Syston North Junction box, seen here a mere five weeks before closure and demolition.

efforts of many thousands of ordinary people that the line is still extant. Undeterred by alarmist and inflated estimates of the cost of repairing and restoring Ribblehead Viaduct and the supposed losses of the line, and disbelieving of the 'expiry date' put on the line and structures by the BR publicity machine, a coalition of local residents and railway enthusiasts lobbied hard and fought the disinformation and refused to let the line die. They did a wonderful job in advertising the plight, putting a stop to the closure plans and attracting new visitors to a wonderful part of the country.

A similar ill-advised closure plan was floated for Marylebone station. In much the same way, closure by stealth was attempted; passenger figures were massaged and all manner of reasons for closure and planned replacements were put forward. But again pressure from the public forced BR to retreat and much-needed investment is now being afforded to this part of the network. (Moreover, steam even returned to the station, despite BR having said for twenty years that this was impossible!)

Other positive signs throughout the decade - and in

many ways it ended as a hopeful ten years - were the re-opening or planned resurrection of lines and stations closed by Beeching, even to the extent of re-boring a tunnel for the line to Mansfield, renovating a line suffering heavily from mining subsidence between Leicester and Burton-on-Trent, and even plans for re-laying the Great Central to either Rugby or Lutterworth - necessitating the re-purchase of land and the re-building of a viaduct. Parkway stations opened in many areas, taking the battle to the car in no uncertain terms; commuter lines such as the Valley lines in South Wales proved that the train can be much faster; 'bustitution' - the crazy plan to substitute loss-making rural services with buses - was seen off, at least in the short-term; and Passenger Transport Authorities and some enlightened Councils saw the great benefits of rail travel and invested accordingly, enabling services to stay open and even new ones to emerge.

The 1980s were of course the decade in which 'green' issues came to the fore. The decade saw at last an awakening and realisation of the damage being done to the planet by pollution and by the car in particular. Virtually everyone agreed on at least one thing, that environmentally railways were a good thing. The perception was promoted with considerable skill by such bodies as the Railway Development Society and Transport 2000, but this awareness created a credibility problem for public policy. Mrs Thatcher's antipathy to railways and her sympathies for the road lobby were perhaps the first elements of her political philosophy to be called into question, but by the end of the decade the debate had moved on. Despite political prevarication which has handicapped BR in such areas as the planning of the route of the Channel Tunnel line, and a generally accepted belief that investment has been starved, there have still been many positive developments. The travelling public still has something approaching a good service and passenger numbers are growing annually, a testament to the skill, ingenuity and sheer devotion of rail workers. They have coped with both their own and their political masters moving the goalposts, and with equipment that is in many instances life expired, and their efforts - often herculean - must be acknowledged by all of us who care for Britain's railways.

With numerous policy changes on engine numbering and naming, often frustrating and infuriating, part-privatisation and the encouraging of private locos/stock to run on the BR network, constant changes in corporate policy, spreading electrification, and freight policies and markets changing, today's railway photographers have to try to capture anything and everything. For those cameramen who can survive the second recession in ten years, there is likely to be much to see and record and a healthy number of outlets to use the end results.

I hope that the images in this book of BR in the 1980s will provide a telling photographic memoir of those interesting years. No one person can hope to do more than scratch the surface of what has happened, so this does not attempt to be a definitive view of the decade; rather, it is a personally selected view of some of the things that have happened and changed in those years, with the emphasis on the aesthetic. It intends to show what has gone, rather than what has taken its place. I apologise if your favourite line or class of loco has been omitted; I trust that you will forgive me, and I hope that you will find these a series of memorable reflections on the years in question.

I have been greatly assisted by four of our finest photographers - Tom Heavyside, Colin Marsden, Brian Morrison and Tom Noble. Without their generous cooperation the collection would have been much the poorer and I record my deep gratitude for their speedy and ready responses to my *cris de coeur*. Their names are credited where appropriate, otherwise the photos are my own.

I also owe much to the patience and tolerance of wife Judith, son Adam and daughter Tammy, for putting up with me constantly disappearing to take photos or having my head buried in railway photographs/magazines/books; I also thank the publishers for their farsightedness and encouragement.

I have derived immense pleasure from wallowing in this recent nostalgia, and if the following pages impart half the pleasure to the reader that I have enjoyed in putting them together, then I shall be satisfied.

**M. John Stretton**

# 1980-1981

**4 March 1980**
As the decade dawned, relatively quietly, none of us could foresee the massive amount of change that would be wrought. It hardly seemed feasible that 'Deltics' would disappear within two years, and many other classes suddenly acquire devotees as they approached extinction.

Class '50s' ended the period much-loved, but in 1980, although of interest as they had only recently been transferred to the Western Region from the West Coast Main Line, they were still relatively unsung. With the skyline of Reading proud in the background, No 50006 *Neptune* heads west past Southcote Junction with the 12.30 Paddington-Plymouth, six months after refurbishment and naming.
*Colin Marsden*

**10 April 1980**
*Left* Another '50', but this time performing on the Waterloo-Exeter route. Whilst many preferred the large-numbered livery of the mid-'eighties, the much more nondescript earlier version was not unattractive and is seen here on No 50042 *Triumph*, passing Surbiton on the last stages of its journey with the 06.15 Exeter-Waterloo. *Colin Marsden*

**13 April 1980**
*Below* Growing up near Leicester, 'Peaks' held a special place in my affections, but to a wider public they were largely unnoticed until their replacement on the Midland Main Line by HSTs in September 1982. As Type 4 mixed-traffic locos, their geographical travels were far and wide, as can be judged by No 45039 *The Manchester Regiment* seen here passing Chepstow on an early morning Sunday Cardiff-Portsmouth Harbour service. *Brian Morrison*

**23 April 1980**
*Below left* How to make a mundane scene interesting. The 16.10 Hexham-Newcastle service pauses at Wylam, on the Northumberland border, with Cravens Class '105' DMU No E56474 framed by the bridge and superb signal box structure. Fifteen months later, this unit was refitted as a Sandite Unit, under Departmental No ADB977049, and had disappeared from active service by the end of the decade. *Tom Heavyside*

*26 April 1980*
The Settle-Carlisle route spent much of the decade in the news, with BR trying desperately to close it, and thousands of fans fighting to save it. Fortunately it survived long enough, due to a combination of happy circumstances and determined opposition, to see a shift in public opinion towards railways and become an idea that met its time. This was not before there had been extensive re-routing of services away from the line, however. One such service, the 09.52 Leicester-Glasgow, enjoys the sunshine at Ais Gill, before the change, behind No 47535. *Tom Heavyside*

*28 April 1980*
One more crossing about to hit the head-lines? Fortunately not, as No 47706 *Strathclyde* is stopped at the signal, west of Falkirk, at the point where the ex-North British Railway crosses the Forth & Clyde Canal, whilst working the 10.05 Glasgow-Edinburgh, diverted via Falkirk Grahamston because of the temporary closure of Falkirk High tunnel. One hopes that the cloth-capped signalman appreciated all the extra work! *Tom Noble*

## Monday, 26 May 1980

The 1980s saw the 150th anniversaries of various parts of the railway system and as a result, alert to the money-making possibilities, BR organised various celebratory events. Amongst the most enjoyable, by virtue of the many ancient locos taking part, was the Rocket 150 celebrations. Ex-LNWR 2-4-0 No 790 *Hardwicke* is most definitely the centre of attraction here, and the focus of many admiring glances, despite the very cold day, as she leaves Bold Colliery and passes through St Helens Junction station, *en route* to the cavalcade. *Tom Heavyside*

## 27 May 1980

What so many of us realised only in retrospect - often when it was too late - was how much of the established railway scene was passing away under our very noses. It had been there for generations and, seemingly, would always be there. Some of the rationalisation at Bishop Auckland can be seen in this view of a Cravens two-car unit (comprising Nos E51482 and E56423) waiting to form the 15.10 service to Darlington. In happier days a web of lines radiated from the town, and until August 1968 those seen here would have continued to Durham, but now some ex-NE station structures have been stripped from the Durham platform, as well as the middle roads, and the whole has a feeling of dilapidation; only the semaphores and signal box give a happy link with the past. *Brian Morrison*

**29 May 1980**
A classic view, another that dramatically altered during the 'eighties. Rationalisation has stripped Newcastle of its diamond crossing and cars now occupy much of the area in the middle-distance - Platforms 1 to 6! Also Class '40s' are now, sadly, only a memory. No 40073, with route discs removed, heads north through the station with an ammonia train. *Brian Morrison*

*4 July 1980*
Another junction, at the other end of the country. Part of the art of successful modern railway photography is getting away from the standard three-quarter view and being adventurous with the lens. How many of us would have thought of capturing the DMU at this point? But it serves to emphasise the loneliness of the branch line, compared to the main line in the foreground. A Gloucester '119' unit forms the 14.10 Truro-Falmouth service, having just left Penwithers Junction, south of Truro. *Brian Morrison*

**21 August 1980**

*Above* Another view unremarkable at the time, a Class '50' in Devon, hauling a top-link Paddington-West of England service. By the end of the decade all such services were HST-covered, but No 50016 *Barham* just managed to see the end of the period, being stopped at Laira in July 1990 with power unit problems and being formally withdrawn on the 10th. Ten years earlier, however, that was still a long way off as the loco rounds Aller Junction with the 11.30 train from London to Penzance. *Colin Marsden*

**3 September 1980**

*Above right* For me, one of the saddest events of the early 1980s was the closure of the Woodhead Tunnel route from Manchester-Sheffield, and the withdrawal of the Class '76' electrics. I fondly remember them gliding around Wath, at the eastern end, and I greatly regret not having seen them at work over the route itself. Often double-headed, they hauled heavy freight back and forth daily, such as this loaded coal train heading westwards through Valehouse, near Woodhead, behind Nos 76010 and 76007. *Brian Morrison*

**4 September 1980**

*Right* Once one of a pair, with its twin at the now extinct ex-Midland station, the delightful fan-tail window at the ex-LNWR terminus at Buxton thankfully still remains. The 'cow-horn' exhausts of Class '128' DPU complete the picture, as No 55990 stands while the parcels are loaded into the specially converted unit. *Brian Morrison*

*6 September 1980*
As the decade opened there was certainly no thought of the 'Peaks' disappearing from the scene within a handful of years. Indeed, even when HSTs later took over on the Midland Main Line, there were plans to prepare some to run into the 'nineties; sadly, this did not happen. In much happier times, and most definitely retaining its character with split-headcodes, a healthy looking No 45120 passes Dronfield, prior to the station's re-opening, at the head of the 10.10 Sheffield-St Pancras express, having just emerged from Broadway Tunnel. *Brian Morrison*

*6 September 1980*
I always wondered how drivers could adequately see over the great nose-ends of 'Deltics'; it must have led to some skilful handling. The driver of No 55008 *The Green Howards* can barely be glimpsed in his cab, as the 11.12 King's Cross-Scarborough service negotiates the cross-over on the exit from Retford station. *Brian Morrison*

**17 September 1980**
The Peak Forest route, near Buxton, lost its passenger services on 1 July 1968, but thanks largely to ICI and stone traffic the line is very much alive and kicking. Motive power and stock changed frequently during the 'eighties, however, with many classes of engine now no longer seen. An example is No 25163, seen approaching Great Rocks Junction with an empty Northwich-Tunstead ICI hopper train. *Tom Heavyside*

**14 March 1981**
Another 'Rat', this time on passenger duty. Before 'Sprinterisation' took over, the Crewe-Cardiff services were formed of comfortable, largely Mark 1 stock, with plenty of space. Here No 25042 is seen only a few miles out of Newport, at Caerleon, with such a train. *Tom Heavyside*

**16 April 1981**
On 17 March 1979 the ex-NBR Penmanshiel Tunnel was closed to all traffic and a diversion was provided. Two years on, No 40057 heads south over the new diversion line with the 17.07 Edinburgh-Newcastle service. *Tom Heavyside*

**20 April 1981**
Some indication of the bulk, power and majesty of the 'Deltics' is apparent from this view of No 55004 *Queen's Own Highlander*, standing under Edinburgh's magnificent train shed, waiting to form the 11.50 to King's Cross. Having ousted Gresley's 'A4s' from the East Coast Main Line some twenty years earlier, it did not seem possible that they in turn would be 'redundant' and discarded within two years of the date of this photograph. No 55004 actually succumbed just seven months later. *Tom Heavyside*

*20 April 1981*
*Left* Marshalling yards are not now what they once were, in the glorious days of humps and constant train reformations. Block trains and company loads ended much of the need for shunting and the demise of Speedlink in 1991 sounded the death knell for many. Millerhill, to the south of Edinburgh, enjoyed fluctuating trade during the 'eighties, but still had a future at this date when No 40187 was photographed entering the yard with a mixed freight from the west. *Tom Heavyside*

*23 April 1981*
*Below left* Definitely the old order on the ECML. Tuxford station has long gone and the site is barely recognisable as No 47405 heads south with the 14.10 York-King's Cross. Already eighteen years old at this time, nine of the first ten Brush Type 4s were given 'celebrity' status over the next few years, with a series of namings. No 47405 (the fifth to be built, in January 1963) became *Northumbria* at Newcastle Central on 28 October 1982, retaining the name until withdrawal in March 1986, but its top-link duties were soon taken over by HSTs. *Colin Marsden*

*27 April 1981*
*Below* The end of the line, in more ways than one. Kilmacolm, the terminus of a once much longer G&SWR branch to Greenock, had seen better days and stood under threat of closure when this photograph was taken, showing it host to a DMU waiting to make the return journey down the branch. The 80 mm lens gives a pleasing touch to the juxtaposition of still-wintery birch, creditably clean DMU set, and mix of wood and stone in the station buildings. The line, from Elderslie No 2 Junction to Kilmacolm, closed on 3 January 1983, but there were efforts at reopening at the end of the decade. *Tom Noble*

**2 May 1981**
The Glasgow-Edinburgh push-pull service received much publicity during the 1980s, not least for hitting animals at speed, but the changes in livery and later operational practice were much quieter! In earlier livery, and looking quite pleasing despite the Corporate Blue, No 47710 *Sir Walter Scott* heads the 10.30 service for Edinburgh past Bishopbriggs oil terminal, on the ex-NBR route out of Queen Street station. *Tom Noble*

**26 May 1981**
Taking successful photographs of SR EMUS is not easy, but two are well captured here at Dover Priory. Class '419' MLV No 68007 stands with a 4CEP, between duties, above '411/2' 4CEP No 411513, which is forming the 12.40 service to Victoria. *Brian Morrison*

*15 June 1981*

The Cornish clayhoods received comparatively little attention until their imminent demise, but they gave sterling service, and sights such as No 47374 heading westwards through Totnes in this early afternoon were once relatively common. Although probably not as practical as their successors, the old hoods did have a definite charm, as seen here. *Colin Marsden*

**22 June 1981**

*Left* The ex-Cambrian line to Pwllheli was threatened with extinction, with the County Council proposing to end the travel facilities of local schoolchildren, the gunpowder works at Penrhyndeudraeth closing and the closure of Barmouth bridge. Fortunately the latter was repaired, and sense and investment was restored to the line, but before all this happened DMU No M51587, in experimental livery, leads the 10.30 Pwllheli-Shrewsbury over the viaduct just south of Penrhyn, with the gunpowder works in the background. *Tom Heavyside*

**22 June 1981**

*Below* The offending bridge at Barmouth is seen here prior to closure for repairs, and whilst being eaten away by marine worm. Its precarious nature is well demonstrated in this view of DMUs forming the 12.40 Shrewsbury-Pwllheli service crossing the bridge. *Tom Heavyside*

**29 June 1981**

*Right* Perhaps the traffic that has suffered most over the decade is coal, not least because of the miners' strike of mid-decade. Many South Wales yards suffered, household colliery names closed, communities in the valleys suffered greatly and sights such as this at Mardy Colliery, Maerdy, became much, much rarer. No 37284 shunts the sidings before preparing to leave with a full train, whilst an ex-BR Class '14' 'Teddybear' languishes, stored, in the background. *Tom Heavyside*

**12 September 1981**

*Below right* To some they were 'Rats' - affectionately, of course - and to others they were under-powered and ineffectual, but certainly by the time the end of the Class '25s' came in March 1987 they had acquired a great deal of affection. When that event was still many years away, No 25113 leads No 25139 into Wellington station with the 10.07 Aberystwyth-Euston through train. Rationalisation and 'progress' can also be seen here, with a buffer-stop serving no purpose (left) and cars parked (right) where the tracks at the entrance to the engine shed once lay. *Brian Morrison*

**16 September 1981**
*Above* With all the play that was made of electrification at the end of the decade, it is often forgotten that some lines were the beneficiaries of much earlier investment. Branches around the Wirral are a case in point, with aged stock to prove it. Here 1938-built Class '503' three-coach EMU with No M29273M leading forms the 12.21 Moorfields-New Brighton service approaching its destination. Attractive in its dated design, the Class was withdrawn, more or less en bloc, at the end of 1984. *Brian Morrison*

**17 September 1981**
*Right* Oh for the days when railways truly served the community and pick-up freights were common sights. More track vandalising can be seen all around No 40182, seen leaving Southport Sidings with the return daily freight for Springs Branch, Wigan. The railmen are a delightful study in the sense of urgency of this type of working! *Brian Morrison*

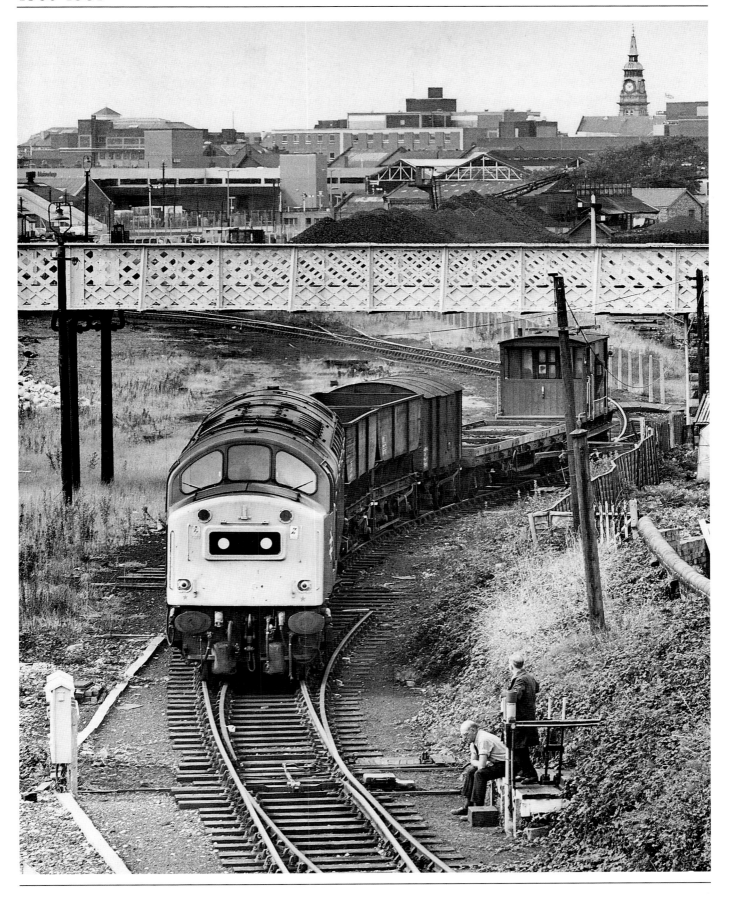

**Sunday 27 September 1981**
The architecture is fascinating and no doubt would send Lucinda Lambton into paroxysms of delight! It also forms a splendid backdrop to No 47378, backing an empty GLC refuse train into the sidings at Southall. The train has emptied Londoners' rubbish into a site at Calvert and has returned via Oxford. Household waste is a growing problem and BR has been able to pick up useful business in other areas, such as Bristol, Manchester and Edinburgh. *Tom Heavyside*

**17 October 1981**
All too soon the last days of the 'Deltics' were on us, all manner of specials were run and thousands of enthusiasts toured the country to catch the last outings. Not surprisingly, and well away from its usual stamping ground, No 55015 *Tulyar* is the subject of much attention, pausing at Eastleigh whilst running the 'Wessex Deltic' railtour. *Colin Marsden*

# 1982-1983

**10 January 1982**
Most of us tend to put away our cameras when the bad weather strikes, but it provides opportunities for different impressions, especially with fog and snow. The latter gives a surreal tinge to even the most common view, and leads to dramatic effects with kicked-up swirls; Class '427' 4VEG No 7907 has obviously met snow *en route*, leaving the driver only a small 'window' to see through and, although slowing for a stop at Clapham Junction, still causes a distinct 'spray' as it brings a Bognor Regis-Victoria service closer to its destination.
*Brian Morrison*

*23 February 1982*
At this stage of the decade it was more usual to see '50s' on passenger workings, but in Cornwall they could be found on all manner of duties. A low weak sun gives a pleasant tinge to No 50043 *Eagle* as it prepares to move past No 37206 out of Truro yard with a distinctly ancient-looking freight for Ponsandane, Penzance. *Brian Morrison*

*17 April 1982*
At the other end of the country a member of another class to be ravaged by withdrawals within just a few years, No 27107, heads north out of Aberdeen, past Kittybrewster, on the old Great North of Scotland Railway route to Inverness. Entering traffic as D5395 in June 1962, allocated to Cricklewood (14A) shed, No 27107 actually spent the majority of its working life in Scotland and was re-numbered five months after this shot, to 27051. Finally withdrawn in July 1987, its last journey was south once more, to be cut up in Vic Berry's famous yard in Leicester in October of that year. *Brian Morrison*

**19 April 1982**
The backlight nicely picks out rails, rocks and roof details in what would otherwise be an ordinary view of an ordinary service train. No 47501, then unnamed but later to be graced with *Craftsman* in 1987, approaches the end of its journey, past Hare Ness, south of Aberdeen, with the 11.35 from Glasgow Queen Street. *Brian Morrison*

**26 April 1982**
As well as locomotives, Vic Berry also dealt a death blow to numerous DMUs, including ex-Swindon Works Class '120'. No 53666 was cut up in April 1986, but in happier times and in its previous incarnation as No 50666, as part of Cardiff's C508 set, it leads the 13.36 service from Birmingham New Street into Great Malvern. The six cars make today's two-car 'Sprinters' look rather meagre! *Tom Heavyside*

**27 April 1982**
*Above left* The sheer size of Severn Tunnel Junction station and the railway land around it give some idea of past importance, and one wonders at the 'politics' and 'logic' involved in reducing the area, and especially the once vital marshalling yards, to a virtual wasteland by the end of the decade. At this date there was, however, still some life in the services, albeit that seemingly only railwaymen are alighting at the station as No 31414 restarts the 13.01 Bristol-Cardiff service. *Tom Heavyside*

**28 April 1982**
*Left* Another view of the Waterloo-Exeter route with a '50', but now adorned in 'large body logo' livery. Still on ex-Southern metals, No 50033 *Glorious* approaches Exeter Central with the 09.10 from London to St Davids, welcomed by the attractive semaphore gantry. *Tom Heavyside*

**29 April 1982**
*Above* It's never quite the same without semaphores. Much delightful railway design has been lost to colour lights, but fortunately not here at Castle Cary, as Departmental DMUs Nos TDB 975540 (ex-W55016 and adapted for use as a route-learning car) and RDW 150266 enter from the Westbury direction forming an Engineer's inspection train. *Tom Heavyside*

**1 May 1982**
*Below*  My favourite 'Peak', No 45007, rounds the curve in bright spring sunshine pulling away from Aller Junction on the main line immediately to the south of Newton Abbot station, heading the 08.15 Birmingham-Plymouth. The semaphores seen in the distance control the Torquay branch. Lasting until the end of the '45s', in 1988, No 45007 (ex-D119 of 1961) was still bodily intact at the end of the decade and it would be nice to think that it could be preserved. *Tom Heavyside*

**28 May 1982**
*Right*  Not inherently aesthetically attractive, it is nevertheless interesting to view development of SR EMU front-end design. '405/2' 4SUB set No 4356 (right) is one of the Southern Railway four-car slam-door suburban units, built at Eastleigh between 1946 and 1951, whereas '423' 4VEP No 7753 (left) is of much later vintage, built as express stock by BR(SR) between 1967 and 1974. Seen in Clapham Cutting, No 7753 heads south-west as the 10.50 Waterloo-Guildford, racing past No 4356 as the 10.46 Waterloo-Wimbledon-Richmond-Waterloo circular service. *Brian Morrison*

**5 June 1982**
*Below right*  Looking for all the world like something created by a highly imaginative and skilled modeller, a very clean and mixed set of DMUs, led by Class '108' No M52043, approaches Chester. When they first appeared, ousting beloved steam engines and services, the 'railcars' were not loved, but thirty years on, with the advent of 'Sprinters' and the rest, that perception has changed to one of affection and much greater appreciation. *Tom Heavyside*

**5 June 1982**
After the 'Deltics', the Class '40s' ('Whistlers') became the enthusiasts' favourites. Judging from the heads poking from the front coach windows, some appreciation of their value is spreading as No 40184 leaves Chester under a most imaginative and delightful LNWR signal box design, hauling the 09.00 York-Llandudno. Withdrawn from Longsight depot in December 1982, No 40184 was finally disposed of at Doncaster Works twelve months later. *Tom Heavyside*

**11 June 1982**
One piece of photographic advice I have been given on numerous occasions is 'put something in the foreground'. Here the single semaphore and small call-on signal turn an ordinary shot into a delight. The old order for coal trains in South Wales is seen in the form of Nos 37295 and 37281 approaching Ystrad Mynach, double-heading an empty merry-go-round train bound for Penallta Colliery from Aberthaw. The line to the right is the branch from Cwm Bargoed DP. *Colin Marsden*

**11 June 1982**
Viewed after change, things sometimes just do not look right! On the face of it, Pontypool has more than its fair share of land for a tiny rural station, but this belies its history.
At its heyday within the GWR, the station served as a focal point for six branches, and carriage sidings and other platforms would have been in use. In 1982, though,
Met-Cam DMU set B810 looks lost as it passes through the station with a special train. *Brian Morrison*

**16 June 1982**
Early in the 'eighties, Scotland seemed largely forgotten and ignored, but as the decade wore on, not least through the magnificent efforts of Scotrail boss Chris Green, the country's railways became both revitalised and a mecca for enthusiasts. Part of the reason for the latter circumstance, Class '37s' on passenger, is evidenced here by No 37012, named *Loch Rannoch* a mere 2½ months earlier, leaving Fort William for Mallaig with the 08.34 service from Glasgow. Nos 37085 and 20191 look on from the Mallaig Junction yard on the left. *Tom Heavyside*

**20 June 1982**
Much has changed at this location over the years, despite its timeless quality. A semaphore signal used to stand by the quarter-milepost, a host of telegraph wires did their graceful dance by the lineside, one of the two slow lines in the foreground was later removed and the alignment slewed towards the bridge, and of course the '45s' have disappeared. Nearing the end of its days as top-link power, No 45122 heads south with a clear road under a leaden sky past Barkby Thorpe, four miles to the north of Leicester, with the 12.00 Sheffield-St Pancras.

*20 June 1982*
Another view drastically altered. By the decade's end this shot would be masked by a growth of bushes, but if they were cleared virtually all that would be seen today would be the flats in the distance and the oil drum in the foreground! The motive power seen here, the

buildings, lights and far sidings have all gone. What was the site of Leicester Midland (15C) shed roundhouse (extreme right) now houses the local area signal power box, but on this day it was home to, among others, Nos 45043 *The King's Own Royal Border Regiment*, 47315, 08618 and 08695.

*14 August 1982*
The blue and grey HST livery has long gone, as has the 'Heart-Line' legend on the power car. The significance of this was unknown to me, but surely cannot refer to the Newcastle-Paignton service that stands in Rotherham station. *Tom Heavyside*

*22 August 1982*
It is only in retrospect that the magnitude of change can be judged. Railway infrastructure that had seemed so permanent often disappeared quietly, but was no less dramatic for all that. At Loughborough the warehouse that so dominates this scene is no more. The signal box has also gone, along with the attendant semaphore signals, '08s' no longer spend time shunting the ARC yard, and the yard trackwork has been slightly rationalised. Fortunately, the Midland origins of the station are still extant, the Brush Works (left) still sees success, and there is a distinct hope that the ex-GCR embankment (right distance) will see tracks again.

*27 August 1982*
March was always a strange place, stuck in the middle of nowhere and yet a magnet for enthusiasts, drawn by the proliferation of freight workings and the ageing DMUs on local services. On the left, Cravens Class '105' No E51284 restarts the 14.30 Cambridge-Lincoln, whilst on the right another '105', No E56468, waits to do the same, forming the 12.40 Doncaster-Ely. Exactly three months later the direct line to Spalding closed, together with these platforms. *Tom Heavyside*

*28 August 1982*
Over the years the cross-country Birmingham-East Anglia services have seen a variety of motive power and fluctuations in fortunes. In the days when decent amounts of passenger space was provided, No 31303 enters Cambridgeshire and Shippea Hill station, just a few miles from Ely, with the 14.14 Norwich-Birmingham service. *Tom Heavyside*

**29 August 1982**
A delightfully rural scene, despite being in Greater London, as Kent Coast express stock 4CEP No 411606 heads for the capital forming a Ramsgate-Victoria train, passing a Maidstone semi-fast at Bickley Junction on the ex-SE&CR line to Bromley. The lines to the right head for Petts Wood and Orpington; ten years on, the left and middle pair of tracks had been joined to give four-track cover for the Bickley-Petts Wood chord. *Brian Morrison*

**August 1982**
Some of the gentility of suburbia is evidenced by the allotments at Chiswick as 2HAP No 6002 (an early casualty to withdrawal only months after this shot) ambles on its unhurried way eastwards from Chiswick & Grove Park station on the ex-LSWR route from Feltham to Barnes via Brentford, forming the 12.28 Twickenham-Waterloo. *Brian Morrison*

**16 September 1982**
Even though they replaced the likes of 'Jubilees', I have always had a soft spot for the 'Peaks' which for many years were the mainstay of the Midland Main Line services out of St Pancras, until finally completely replaced by HSTs in mid-decade. Not spectacular in the way of the 'Deltics', they were good, honest, reliable workhorses, and it was sad to see them go. Two years prior to their ousting, No 45132 looks good as it pulls northwards out of Derby bound for Leeds. *Tom Heavyside*

**21 September 1982**
Another scene that is no more. Between shunting duties at the ill-fated Shildon Works, Nos 08268 and 08063, with three and two years of life left respectively, stand in the autumn sunshine, apparently of no interest to the pub-painters! *Tom Heavyside*

**23 September 1982**
*Above*  This picture has so much of interest, including one of the reasons for some retained use of the Settle-Carlisle line - the MOD need for the Warcop branch from Appleby. With a long consist of ammunition, whose sheer uniformity has aesthetic value - and a barrier wagon! - No 40080 heads away from the branch at Keld, south of Appleby, with some of the dramatic moodiness of the S&C apparent in the background. *Tom Heavyside*

**21 October 1982**
*Above right*  Many railway photographers shy away from night-time shots, but they are surprisingly easy, as the film tolerance is exceptional; and they do often make for very pleasing views. A sight to be seen no more, under normal circumstances, is a '47' heading west from Swansea. No 47565 waits for its driver before setting off as the 20.18 service to Milford Haven. *Tom Heavyside*

**22 November 1982**
*Right*  As well as the Settle-Carlisle line, there was a battle royal over Marylebone. To justify almost anything, usage figures for the station, as quoted by BR, fluctuated wildly, and this did not help the campaigners, who were adamant that it should stay open. The poster's message does seem to give an over-optimistic view of the problem, but to their great credit those campaigners did win the day and the two businessmen could look forward to strolling these platforms for many years to come.

**7 February 1983**
The infamous Ribblehead Viaduct, from a slightly unusual angle. Typical winter weather for the S&C almost creates a white-out on Whernside in the background as both photographer and No 40152 brave the cold and discomfort, the latter hauling a load from Ribblehead Quarry. The engine will run round its train at Horton, before returning through Ribblehead in the up direction, bound for Healey Mills. *Brian Morrison*

**9 February 1983**
Yes, I am biased, but railways are a much less wasteful user of precious land than motorways, and to my mind the Lune Gorge proves this. Some of the rape of the area by the M6 can be seen in the background, as No 87013 *John O'Gaunt* weaves its way past Grayrigg with the southbound 09.37 Carlisle-Euston InterCity service. The arctic conditions of the previous view are obviously still around, despite the weak winter sun. *Brian Morrison*

**9 February 1983**
Another interesting night-time shot, with the station lights picking out the infrastructure details at Lancaster, as No 47455 pauses with the 17.53 Workington-Huddersfield TPO. *Brian Morrison*

*26 March 1983*
Yet more vanished infrastructure, and another view of the location on page 41 (upper). So much of this scene also is no more, not least the sidings in the left and middle distance, the box and signals. The view north from Leicester now looks so bare, and it is highly unlikely that Class '31s' will be seen on regular passenger workings again. No 31423 approaches London Road station in charge of the 09.49 Norwich-Birmingham (New Street) cross-country service. *Brian Morrison*

**9 April 1983**
Distant views often fail to succeed, but here Stokesay Castle has been well used in juxtaposition with the flat open countryside and the Malverns as a backdrop, to give a frame for No 47257 as it heads south with a Manchester-Bristol parcels train. *Tom Heavyside*

**22 April 1983**
Somehow I never visited Broad Street in steam days, although it was next door to Liverpool Street station, and I only came to know it in its terminal years, so to speak. It was a haven of peace and tranquillity in a very busy area of London, and was like stepping into the past. EMU set No 501178, with coach M75178 leading, is part of all this, still in all-Corporate Blue, waiting to form the 16.41 train to Watford. By this time services had been truncated to the extent that half of the station platform area (to the left of this view) had been taken over by what appeared to be triffids, and access to the station was by way of side stairs.

*22 April 1983*
Next door, at Liverpool Street, modernisation is advancing, with the ubiquitous overhead wires and a newer-generation unit entering with a commuter train. The spotters on the left, however, appear to have other things on their minds.

22 April 1983
By the end of the decade 'Heritage' first-generation DMUs were being replaced in great numbers, but many were still giving sterling service. One line that was fairly late in receiving improvements was that to Aylesbury out of Marylebone. When largely ignored by photographers, especially in the pouring rain as here, Class '115' units arrive at Amersham with the 17.42 commuter service from the capital to Aylesbury.

**26 April 1983**
Being by nature mixed-traffic locos, certainly in their later years, '45/46s' could turn up on a wide variety of duties. Still with some pride, No 45063 heads north towards Taunton with an express parcels train. *Tom Heavyside*

**29 April 1983**
Much was made towards the end of the decade of the weedkiller trains hauled by specially converted Class '20s', but the idea was nothing new, as evidenced by No 37207 *William Cookworthy* rounding the curve of the branch from Boscarne Junction with the Chipman train, about to meet up with the main line at Bodmin Road. *Tom Heavyside*

*30 April 1983*
At the other end of one of the lines from
Broad Street, a '501' unit waits for departure to a different destination. Standing in
the suburban platforms at Watford
Junction, showing buildings that were
swept away a matter of weeks after this
photograph was taken, still all-blue No
501153 waits to leave as the 10.25 2nd-
class-only stopper to Euston, with the driver
approaching, but apparently of no interest
to a young Tammy Stretton!

*7 May 1983*
Trackwork around the Wakefield area has seen much rationalisation and down-grading, not all of it advisable or successful, and one
point to suffer reversal of fortune and drastic indignity in the 'eighties was Goose Hill Junction, Normanton. Incredibly it was the ex-
MR main line from Leeds to Sheffield and Rotherham that was sacrificed (seen here as the left-hand route), with the ex-L&Y 'deviation'
line via Barnsley remaining open. Before this desecration, No 31324 comes off the ex-L&Y line and heads past the attractive box and
semaphore gantry - both now gone - with an eastbound engineer's train. *Tom Heavyside*

**14 May 1983**
Another view of Clapham Junction (see page 37), with this time No 508005 heading south on the ex-LSWR lines as the 10.35 Waterloo-Chessington South service, and passing '421/1' 4CIG No 7313 going the other way on ex-LB&SCR tracks, heading for Victoria station as a service from Brighton. Originally built as four-car units, as seen here, the '508s' were subsequently deprived of a trailer, renumbered and transferred north for Merseyrail duties, with No 508005 becoming 508105 of Birkenhead depot. *Brian Morrison*

**14 June 1983**

If nothing else, the Victorian engineers crafted some magnificent structures, whether they were tunnels, train sheds or viaducts. Though not as famous as some others, the Cynghordy viaduct, on the 'Heart of Wales' line, has a distinct charm with its uniform and attractively edged arches, dwarfing the ageing two-car DMU forming the 10.50 Shrewsbury-Swansea service. *Tom Heavyside*

**15 June 1983**

The dimensions of the Burry Port & Gwendraeth Valley Railway were such that BR locos had to be cut down to work the branch. Cwm Mawr Colliery was the reason for the branch surviving into the decade, when Nos 03145 and 03141, suitably adapted, were used, as seen here passing Pontyates with empties for the colliery. These two engines survived until July 1985, when they were sold, as going concerns, to White Wagtail Ltd, in Coventry. *Tom Heavyside*

**16 June 1983**

To see the decline and eventual closure of Swindon Works during the 'eighties was one of the saddest events of the period. That once proud institution, with its revered 'A' Shop, boasted a work-force of tremendous skill and pride in quality, but was discarded like a wasted asset - a decision still despised by many to this day. The writing was on the wall, with run-down already in train, when a group of bankers enjoyed a private visit. Some can be seen walking away from No 37167, standing outside 'A' Shop, awaiting attention for a missing buffer.

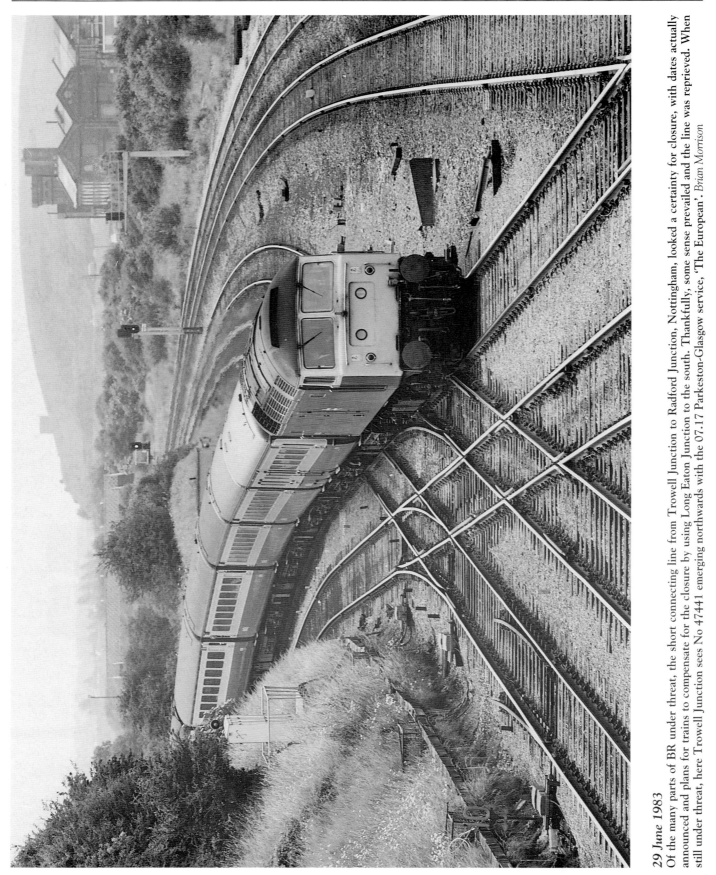

**29 June 1983**
Of the many parts of BR under threat, the short connecting line from Trowell Junction to Radford Junction, Nottingham, looked a certainty for closure, with dates actually announced and plans for trains to compensate for the closure by using Long Eaton Junction to the south. Thankfully, some sense prevailed and the line was reprieved. When still under threat, here Trowell Junction sees No 47441 emerging northwards with the 07.17 Parkeston-Glasgow service, 'The European'. *Brian Morrison*

*30 June 1983*
A child of the 1955 Modernisation Plan, the Class '20s' ('Choppers') obviously had steam ancestry, with the cab at one end facing a 'boiler'. Early on they were 'tandemed'; although pairings were not permanent, solo workings became very much the exception. Midlands coal traffic for power stations, from a base at Toton, was the Class's staple diet and one of these workings is seen at Clay Cross Junction behind Nos 20208 and 20032. A recent transfer south from Scotland is evidenced on the former by the snowploughs - not a common feature on this Class. *Brian Morrison*

*1 July 1983*
Early in 1992 it was announced that the line from Leicester to Burton-on-Trent (the 'Ivanhoe Line') was to be re-opened for passenger traffic. Just how much attention and re-investment would be needed to bring the route up to the necessary standard can be judged from this stretch at Moira West, on the Leicestershire/Derbyshire border. Original blue-liveried No 56051 runs the switchback, caused by mining subsidence, with an empty merry-go-round train from Drakelow to Coalfields Farm. *Colin Marsden*

### 6 July 1983
Although renovated at Brush mid-way through their careers, the '46s' were non-standard, and therefore anathema to BR in the 'eighties; they were thus withdrawn much earlier than their sister Class '45s'. No 46026 *Leicestershire and Derbyshire Yeomanry*, still with nameplates, looks in fine form, however, as it hauls a south-bound HTV train past York, Dringhouses yard. *Colin Marsden*

### 14 July 1983
Not only did the locos receive new coats during the decade, but so did much other rolling-stock. Royal Mail stock was given a complete external overhaul at the end of the period, depriving us of the attractive two-tone livery seen here behind No 45140 at Exeter. At the head of the 19.22 Penzance-Paddington TPO, the '45' would come off at Bristol, probably to be relieved by a '47'. *Colin Marsden*

*18 July 1983*
Another view of the what was left of the once superb Broad Street train shed, with what seems to be a rather inappropriate advert in the background. No 501151, with M75151 leading, is already ten minutes late, according to the clock, as it is scheduled to form the 11.35 to Richmond. *Brian Morrison*

**19 July 1983**
End of the line, and one of Michael Palin's favourite stations! In the days when there was still variety in the Highlands, No 26032 stands in Kyle of Lochalsh station, waiting for passengers from the Skye ferry, to go forward as the 11.10 service to Inverness. Interestingly, the preceding October a car company, Toyota, had brought steam back to the terminus, in conjunction with its promotion of new models on the Isle of Skye! *Tom Heavyside*

**3 August 1983**
Also by the sea, and while not exactly Dawlish, railway holidaymakers can still derive pleasure from sand and rail at Leigh-on-Sea, at least until the tide comes rushing in to rescue the beached vessel *Bembridge*! Two ER '302' EMU sets, with No 302302 leading, seem to be in a hurry to pass the water's edge as they form the 15.12 Fenchurch St-Shoeburyness service, on my 40th birthday. *Brian Morrison*

**6 August 1983**
A delightful view of the sort of railway architecture that was once taken so much for granted, with the exception of the overhead cabin. The line, too, was of the same kind, but soon to lose its services and cease to be part of the East Coast Main Line; the box on the left is already closed. How many, I wonder, would have thought to snap HST No 43087 at that point, as it heads over Selby Swing Bridge with the 17.55 York-King's Cross train, but it is just right. *Tom Heavyside*

*Sunday, 14 August 1983*
*Left* Another view of the electrification that the Mersey system has known for many years. Still displaying great style (not least because of the design's 1938 ancestry) despite the Corporate Blue, Class '503' MBS No M28392M stands in Birkenhead Central ready to take its train to Rock Ferry. *Tom Heavyside*

*17 August 1983*
*Below left* A slightly unusual view of Acton yard, on the Great Western Main Line, but certainly a more unusual motive power on an ex-Paddington local service. Rather than the more conventional DMU, No 210002, one of only two experimental units, heads the 13.05 train to Slough past the healthily stocked yard. *Brian Morrison*

*29 August 1983*
One of the features of the decade, following the sudden reversal of the decision concerning Marylebone, was the resurrection of steam to BR main lines, with one of the most popular of the early series of excursions being the circular 'Scarborough Spa Express' from York. Standing under the superb arched roof of that station, restored 'Black Five' No 5305 waits for the off. Unfortunately the engine failed just five miles out of the city, and had to be rescued by *Evening Star*!

*1 September 1983*
The imposing London office blocks dominate as they look down on and contrast with much earlier architectural styles, and this contrast is echoed in the units on the rails. On the left, slim-bodied Hastings line unit No 1002 forms the 12.45 Charing Cross–Hastings, racing later-designed '415/1' 4EPB No 5140, forming the 12.44 Charing Cross–Orpington, past Waterloo East. *Brian Morrison*

**7 September 1983**

The well-loved institution that was the Cornish clayhoods was a definite link with working practices of the past. It has to be said that the replacement stock exercises greater control of *en route* dust, but the old 'uns had style. In happier times, No 47205 heads a down special of empties, approaching the Exeter Bypass in the late morning. *Colin Marsden*

**7 September 1983**
There cannot be many railway enthusiasts that do not know the South Devon sea-walls, from pictures if not from personal experience, but I would venture that the reversed applies for those who have seen Class '33s' on passenger workings there. Employed due to shortages of DMU stock, prior to the introduction of 'Pacers', the Class was used for a time on Exeter-Paignton locals. No 33058 approaches Teignmouth with the 14.25 service. *Colin Marsden*

**22 October 1983**
Another '33', but this time decidedly cramped for space. The route to Weymouth Quay, through the streets of the town, had been under attack for many years and by the end of the decade was disused. Road traffic was a problem and there appears to be some consternation as to the clearance for No 33112 as it brings the 09.35 Waterloo-Weymouth Quay into its destination, to link up with the ferries to Cherbourg and the Channel Islands. *Brian Morrison*

# 1984-1985

**28 March 1984**

*Above* I don't know how much it cost Brian Morrison to bribe BR for this shot (!), but the chances of this happening again must be millions to one. Despite pouring rain, he has created an incredibly imaginative picture, even with the aperture at f2, showing 4TC No 409 being propelled under Battledown Flyover, at Worting Junction, Basingstoke, by No 33113, forming the 13.10 Salisbury-Waterloo, whilst two 4VEPs speed past with the 12.42 Waterloo-Bournemouth and the 12.12 Bournemouth-Waterloo services. *Brian Morrison*

**1 April 1984**

*Above right* A last look at the '501s' before their demise. It is more usual to see trains climbing Camden Bank out of Euston, and the effects in steam days could be truly impressive. The combination of electricity and descending the bank take away this bonus, but No 501159 still looks attractive under the wires, running as the 12.05 Watford-Euston. *Brian Morrison*

**24 April 1984**

*Right* Another clever use of an 'alternate' vantage point to achieve a much improved picture. An unidentified '45' crosses the graceful, but from this angle delicate-looking, Moorswater Viaduct, Liskeard, with the remains of an earlier structure clearly visible. Passing near the point where the Looe branch loops round and under the main line, the train is an up service from Penzance. *Tom Heavyside*

*29 April 1984*
One consequence of the 1984 miners' strike was the brief cessation of trains on the Chinnor branch, in Oxfordshire. The position was never quite the same again afterwards, and '31s' ceased to stand over the weekend at Aylesbury, as No 31107, one of the early 'crewcut' type still displaying the original siting of nose-doors, is doing in the Sunday morning sunshine. Built by Brush in 1959 as D5525 (Works No 124), it was still going strong over thirty years later, allocated to Bescot.

*3 May 1984*
During the 'eighties, the size and weight of freight trains grew, both as a result of policy, in trying to cut down on the movement of small 'uneconomical' loads, and the development of new rolling-stock, and double-heading was not uncommon. The stone workings for ARC and Foster Yeoman at Westbury provided much welcome revenue for BR, and before the advent of Class '59s' which revolutionised so many duties, Nos 56043 and 56040 *Oystermouth*, still in original livery, are seen on the 10.20 Purfleet-Westbury empties, a regular double-headed job, passing West Ealing. *Colin Marsden*

*23 May 1984*
Other duties for '31s' that suffered in the decade (see opposite) were the Trans-Pennine services to and from Manchester. No 31429 looks very clean and presentable in Piccadilly station before turning out on the 13.41 train to Hull. It is nice to see the amount of ex-LNWR architecture still extant, despite the advent of electrification. *Tom Heavyside*

*7 June 1984*
One more scene that cannot be re-created. The bufferstop concourse at Paddington has changed out of all recognition since this photograph was taken, and the whole station has a much gloomier air than that seen here. Showing off the 'large body logo' livery to advantage - the one I still think was by the far the most suited to them - No 50004 *St Vincent* rests at the terminus after bringing in an express from the West. Entering service in December 1967, the ex-D404 spent most of its life allocated to Laira, having been transferred to the Western Region from Crewe in 1974. It received crests above the name-plates during the late 'eighties, before succumbing to problems early in 1990 and languishing at Laira depot for several months before being withdrawn in June of that year.

**10 July 1984**
Two more '50s' showing off their bulk and power in that livery - they never looked the same engines in Network SouthEast livery, which many of wore in the later years of the decade. Nos 50043 *Eagle* and 50011 *Centurion* look truly majestic as they accelerate away from Bodmin Parkway with the 12.00 Penzance-Glasgow parcels after a scheduled stop for loading. *Centurion* achieved some notoriety

in 1987 when it became the first of the Class to be withdrawn, on 20 February, a victim of accumulated TOPS hours of 8,000-plus, a transfer of repairs to the Class from Doncaster to Crewe, and the need for a static test bed for the Class '50' power units. Interestingly, the loco worked its way to its deathbed at the head of the 1S15 12.15 Penzance-Glasgow as far as Crewe! *Brian Morrison*

**13 July 1984**
Ness Viaduct as it will never look again. The arches under the loco and first coach were swept away by floods at around 08.30 on 7 February 1989, leaving services severely disrupted and locos and stock isolated in the far north of Scotland. The arch under the third coach collapsed at around 18.30 and by midnight only the farthest arch remained. Fortunately, that event is a long way off as No 26035 crosses with the 17.55 Inverness-Kyle of Lochalsh train. *Tom Noble*

**17 July 1984**
One of *the* most interesting events of the decade was the specially staged demonstration test collision with a CEGB nuclear flask at Old Dalby. Like millions of others, I could only watch on television and marvel at the drama and spectacle. The demise of No 46009 was truly spectacular, and here Colin Marsden has superbly captured the very moments of impact, as the 'Peak' literally ploughs (unmanned!) into the flask at virtually 100 mph and the Mark 1 coach behind begins to buckle.

Seconds later, bogies climb into the air as the train powers past the flask and into the trackbed, lost in the smokescreen. Does the world really have a greater sense of security? *Colin Marsden*

**1 August 1984**
Throughout the decade there were many and varied celebrations for anniversaries that seemed to crop up with amazing regularity. One that was slightly different from the rest was the 150th anniversary of Wilsons Brewery in the North West. A number of runs were made by preserved Webb 'Coal Tank' No 1054 (BR No 58926), radiating from Manchester Victoria, where it is seen returning bunker first.

**10 August 1984**
Although limited in number compared to the two distinct alternatives, dual-powered diesel/electric locos and units had a real advantage if there were power failures or if their trains were running to or on non-electrified lines. Due to arcing problems, which had caused No 73142 *Broadlands* to burn out, some Victoria-Gatwick Airport services on this day were entrusted to diesel power. One such, the 11.15 out of London, passes East Croydon behind Nos 73111 and 73117 (later to be named *University of Surrey*). *Brian Morrison*

**11 August 1984**
To me, a loco and coaches is still preferable to a 'Sprinter', from both aesthetic and comfort points of view, but not economically according to BR. In the days when they could still be enjoyed, No 31440 passes Wennington Junction box (although Wennington no longer had a junction) with the 13.36 Lancaster-Hull service. *Tom Heavyside*

**23 August 1984**
Another joy no longer with us is the sight of Class '33s' on inter-regional freight workings. On ex-GWR metals, Nos 33035 and 33111 double-head a 'down' Speedlink freight through Taplow.

**August 1984**
One more example of the skilled photographer's art. Putting the signal box in the foreground makes this picture; sadly this cannot be repeated, as the box has now gone and the location has become rather deserted-looking. HST power car No 43138 heads the 12.50 Plymouth-Paddington past Clink Road Junction, Frome. *Brian Morrison*

**30 August 1984**
Looking back over the decade can become a liturgy of things that have gone, many of them for ever. This siding has now gone and the train no longer runs, but here No 33052 has a very healthy consist of sand as it strives to climb out of the branch from British Industrial Sand at Holmethorpe yard, to run just a mile or so to Redhill yard. *Colin Marsden*

**1 September 1984**
Yet another '33', this time on the 'Severn-Solent' run, prior to the introduction of 'Sprinters' towards the end of the decade. No 33031 heads north on the single track stretch from Yeovil, at Cockhill, near Castle Cary, with the 10.20 Weymouth-Cardiff. *Colin Marsden*

**3 September 1984**
*Above left* An interesting contrast of motive power! It would be fascinating to know the thoughts of the cyclist, patiently waiting for his train, as he closely observes No 43127 heading a Bristol-bound service through Taplow.

**15 October 1984**
*Above* For many years BRCW Class '104' DMUs were the staple diet of the Gospel Oak-Barking service, over the old Tottenham & Hampstead Joint line, but despite their age (or because of it?) and their plain appearance they still had charm. They have now gone, as have the signal box and semaphores, seen here as DMCL No E53492 and DMBS No E53437 approach Upper Holloway with the 14.45 train. *Brian Morrison*

**2 November 1984**
*Left* The water looks cold even on a sunny day! My only visit to Stranraer was in steam days and it was bitterly cold then - that was before the direct line from Carlisle was severed west of Dumfries and all traffic forced to travel via Ayr. Here No 08591 shunts empty car carriers and an oil tank, near the loading bay in Stranraer Harbour, years before voices began to suggest a re-opening of that direct link. *Tom Heavyside*

**16 February 1985**
A fine example of how to use snow, sun and surroundings to turn a potentially ordinary shot into a very pleasing one. The silhouettes of foliage and lamp standard make a very attractive frame for unpretentious Cardiff DMU set C313 as it enters Stroud with a Gloucester-Swindon local service. *Tom Heavyside*

*12 March 1985*
Too far away for us to eavesdrop on the conversation, the effects of light and shade compensate. Escaping for an hour or two from a Ten-Pin Bowling tour, I spent time at both Manchester Victoria and Piccadilly stations. At the former, Parcels van M55993, in the all-Corporate Blue but destined to be transformed into Post Office red three or four years later, stands in the terminal platforms, awaiting the next call of duty.

*16 March 1985*
The destination blind states 'Shaw via Oldham' and this places us unequivocally on the ex-L&Y 'circular' route from Manchester Victoria to Rochdale via Shaw & Crompton. BRCW Class '104' No M53468, 1959 vintage, heads the 16.00 ex-Victoria at Heyside, nearing its destination. Having given reliable service, with very little amendment since construction, the unit just celebrated its thirtieth year, being withdrawn in 1989. *Tom Heavyside*

**28 March 1985**
Semaphores have improved countless railway photographs and this gantry, at the southern exit to Taunton station, was sadly missed when it was dismantled not so long after this view. Thankfully, GUV ('General Utility Van') trains survived the decade, as did No 47306, which had the distinction of being unofficially named *Goshawk* at Tinsley depot on 20 December 1989, just within our time span. Here the Brush Type 4 heads the 05.05 Paddington-Plymouth van train. *Brian Morrison*

**6 April 1985**

*Right* This year saw a shift of thinking by the BR hierarchy away from the obsession with everything looking the same drab blue. That shift, slow as it was at first, gave us no idea of the rainbow of colour/livery changes that were to come, nor of the pace of the change. Repainted in the early ideas for InterCity livery - with sensibly sized numbers - No 86253 *The Manchester Guardian* enters Watford Junction with the 10.06 Euston-Manchester Piccadilly. Note that at this time the coaches are still uniform blue/grey.

**9 April 1985**

*Left* The 'Marlow Donkey' is alas not what it was. Never a long train, a three-car DMU or two single cars as here do not have the same appeal as in steam days, and even the variety of L130's 'cow horn' exhaust pipes cannot compensate completely. No W55030 leads into Bourne End, once a through station on the ex-GWR Maidenhead-High Wycombe branch but now 'terminalised', before reversing to gain the branch line to Marlow, seen swinging to the right behind the unit.

**10 April 1985**

Before the project was scrapped, I wanted to see the APT, so found out the times of its test runs. Short of available spare time through domestic duties, I set up on Tring station to wait. It was late, and I did not see it, except from the car as I drove away, but I was compensated before I left by this view of an '81', then a Class becoming much rarer on main-line working. No 81005 does not seem overburdened on an up parcels passing through Tring at around 13.00.

**10 April 1985**
Later that day I tried again to capture the APT on its return journey north. Being later arriving at a bridge south of Tring station than I had wanted, the train arrived at virtually the same time. I had no time to do other than point the camera through the car window and fire! Not a brilliant shot, admittedly, but my only view of the 'tilting train', and a memorable experience.

**11 April 1985**
For twenty years Class '27s' gave sterling service in Scotland, but did not survive through the decade to 1989. Some, however, escaped the cutter's torch by preservation, and one such is No 27059, here running behind No 27026 in normal service as 'super-power' for an up empty bitumen tanks train from Culloden, seen running through Blair Atholl station on the old Highland Railway route from Perth to Inverness. *Tom Heavyside*

*24 April 1985*
If you can turn your eye away from the front-three-quarter view, and can use the infrastructure, you can create some memorable shots, especially if the sun shines. Ace photographer Brian Morrison has captured this delightful study of a tablet exchange at Tunbridge Wells West B signal box in the bright sunshine, with DEMU No 1305 about to pass the box forming the 14.57 Eridge-Tonbridge. *Brian Morrison*

*27 April 1985*
The blue and white coaches and colour lights give the game away a little, but this is virtually a timeless view for any period since Nationalisation, showing just what can be achieved by preservation. British Railways green-liveried No 60009 *Union of South Africa* - perhaps just a little too clean for purists - heads past Edinburgh Princess Street Gardens on one of a series of round trips around the city via the suburban line. *Tom Heavyside*

*3 May 1985*
Tunnels and cuttings add problems for successful railway photography, but also add challenge and potential. The latter is well encapsulated in this view of No 47409 entering Liverpool Lime Street with the 10.00 Trans-Pennine service from Scarborough, just four months before being given *David Lloyd George* nameplates by David Penhaligan MP at King's Cross on 14 September, prior to working a Pullman special to the Liberal Party Assembly at Dundee. The naming was short-lived, as the engine was withdrawn on 31 August 1986. *Tom Heavyside*

**1 June 1985**
*Above left*  Reading Open Day was graced with brilliantly sunny and hot weather, and as with any Open Day there were a goodly number of surprises and interesting things to see. Encapsulating both is No 31158, in the new Railfreight livery that had been launched without ceremony a mere three months earlier, showing off the depot's loco hoist.

**15 June 1985**
*Left*  The North London line to North Woolwich achieved greater status towards the end of the decade, following the closure of the Dalston West Junction-Broad Street 'branch' and the opening of the Docklands Light Railway. More trains then ran from Richmond to the Eastern terminus than previously, but that is still to come as '416/3' 2EPB unit No 6318 (ex-No 5660 of 1958) waits to form the 11.37 service to Richmond, whilst a 1942-vintage Peckett saddle tank simmers quietly in the yard of the Great Eastern Railway Museum in the background. *Brian Morrison*

**16 June 1985**
*Above*  By the middle of the year, the Victoria-Gatwick 'Railair' link had become well established, with Class '73s' being dedicated to the service and being re-liveried. No 73122 - in trouble earlier in the year at Eastbourne, derailed up to its bogies in ballast - is seen in revised Executive livery at Victoria, waiting to take the 16.00 train to Gatwick. Exactly one month later the engine was named *County of East Sussex*, and was earmarked to be the second Royal '73' locomotive, sharing duties with No 73142 *Broadlands*.

**18 July 1985**

I've said it before, but oh for the days of long loco-hauled trains! The porter seems particularly uninterested, and is obviously not aware of what would disappear so soon, as No 45141 powers the ten-coach 1V81 09.17 Leeds-Penzance train through Totnes. Not surviving the decade - being withdrawn on 4 August 1988 - the '45' did have a brief moment of glory, being endowed with the unofficial name *Zephyr* at Tinsley on 13 August 1987. *Brian Morrison*

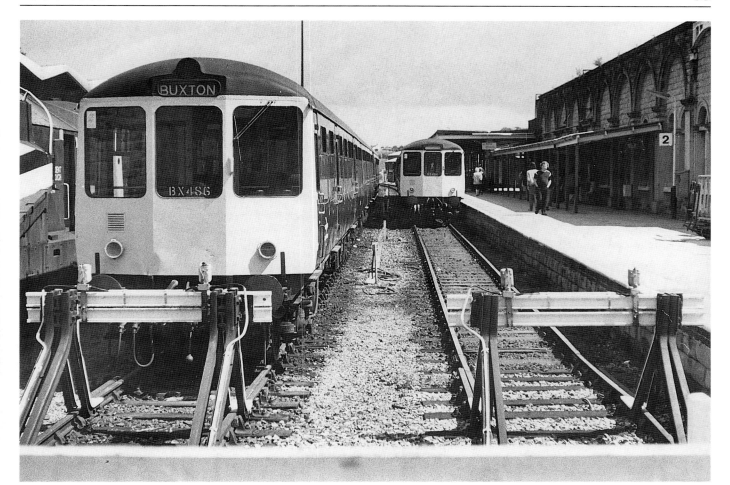

**21 July 1985**
Buxton became something of a mecca for enthusiasts during the mid-'eighties, to view the stronghold of Class '104' DMUs. Approaching their thirtieth birthday, they were still giving sterling work and still looked smart in the sunshine, despite their advancing years and the by then out-of-date and unloved all-over blue livery. No M53427 of set BX486 (on the left) and No M53474 of BX480 (right) are both temporarily at rest before resuming their trips to Manchester Piccadilly.

**1 August 1985**
During the decade the ex-GWR Paddington-Birmingham main line, via High Wycombe, used DMUs exclusively on passenger work-ings with the exception of one loco-hauled train in both directions between Wolverhampton and London. For the two years that I worked in Flackwell Heath I was able to see the morning up service (06.22 ex-Wolverhampton) on my way to work, and to enjoy the one sight of Class '50s' on the line. On the climb out of High Wycombe the engines had to work hard, and No 50015 *Valiant* leans into the camber at Loudwater, determined not to lose time.

*4 September 1985*
*Above left* As well as loco-hauled stock disappearing, long trains of any description were becoming rare creatures. Not so here, as slim-line Class '202' Hastings DEMUs Nos 1012 and 1016 approach Chislehurst on the old SE&CR route to the south, forming the 09.15 Charing Cross-Hastings service. *Brian Morrison*

*6 September 1985*
*Left* The natural temptation would have been to get closer to the line and focus on the DMU, but 'stepping back' and incorporating the debris of the coastline makes for a far more interesting view. The low sun is also well used, and makes for a very pleasing photograph of a Carlisle-Barrow service, near Netherton on the Cumbrian Coast route. *Tom Heavyside*

*26 September 1985*
*Above* SR EMUs spent much of the later parts of the 'eighties being shuffled, re-arranged, refurbished and re-numbered, and it became almost impossible to keep up with it all! Where 'sets' could not be made or maintained, hybrid sets appeared, and one such, 7700, made up of spare VEP and CIG cars 76690 (ex-7840), 62200 (7739), 70798 (7718) and 76639 (7365), forms the 10.28 train to Reading from Waterloo.

3 October 1985
Another '50', but now the coaching stock is dwindling. Supports for Brunel's original viaduct can still be seen, now claimed by nature, as No 50003 *Temeraire* crosses the later version at Coombe St Stephen, near Liskeard, with the 11.28 Plymouth-Penzance train. *Brian Morrison*

**4 October 1985**
'Cornish Railways' is the legend on the nose of No 37196 *Tre Pol and Pen* as it approaches Lostwithiel with the Goonbarrow-Carne Point clay hoods train. Once again the photographer has made excellent use of a semaphore, the hoods themselves, the train's position, a 180 mm lens and, above all, light direction to make a truly evocative scene.
*Brian Morrison*

# 1986-1987

**3 January 1986**
*Above* The delightful use of natural framing and perspective has again turned an ordinary scene into an aesthetic pleasure. With only five years of life left, before the service was turned over to Light Rail operation, the 12.45 Bury-Manchester Victoria service crosses Radcliffe Viaduct. *Tom Heavyside*

**4 February 1986**
*Above right* Whilst standardisation is nothing new to the railways, the ideas behind the Class '58s', with their modular concept, were supposed to be a pointer to the future. For whatever reason, this thinking did not totally succeed with the Class, with later loco builds reverting to older practices. When Doncaster Works (later re-named BRML) was still building new stock, the cab ends of No 58042, with new-style vents, stand in No 4 Bay, awaiting attention. *Colin Marsden*

**24 March 1986**
*Right* As coal traffic changed dramatically over the decade due to the miners' strike, as previously mentioned, closure of collieries and the introduction of merry-go-round trains and new rolling-stock, so did the work of stone trains. In the days of PGAs and '56s', No 56033 rounds the curve at Clink Road Junction with a stone train from ARC Whatley Quarry bound for Eastleigh (see also page 78). *Colin Marsden*

## 26 March 1986
*Left* To my mind surely one of the most aesthetically pleasing of all EMU designs, the Class '310s' gave many years of loyal service on the WCML. Largely ignored by enthusiasts more interested in the loco-hauled trains on the fast lines, there is still charm in the 'hum-drum', as shown by No 310 090 arriving at Hemel Hempstead to pick up passengers for the 09.37 Birmingham-Euston service. The unit was later refurbished and renumbered, as 310105, to concentrate its work around the West Midlands.

## 16 April 1986
*Below left* The introduction to the country of Class '59s' (see overleaf) brought great changes to the Merehead trains. Prior to that '56s' generally held sway, and here No 56033 is seen again (see page 99), this time on a down service to Merehead Quarry as the ex-10.05 empties train from Acton. *Colin Marsden*

## 10 May 1986
*Below* The Venice-Simplon Orient Express set of Pullman cars did many journeys around the southern half of the country in the later years of the decade and entertained thousands of satisfied customers. During 1986 the VSOE 'Bournemouth Belle' continued to operate and is seen, complete with glorious headboard and appropriate headcode, at West Byfleet, headed by No 33111. *Colin Marsden*

**13 May 1986**

*Above left* Way out, indeed! Such was the comment from many a railwayman about the 'Quiet Americans'. Built at General Motors' La Grange workshops in Illinois and shipped to this country aboard a Dutch freighter, they certainly proved to be a revolution in locomotive design and performance, and made BR sit up and take notice. Owned by Foster Yeoman, for use on their stone trains out of Merehead, they impressed all who saw them. No 59002 (then still un-named) heads east through Hungerford station in the late afternoon sun at the head of the 17.05 ex-Merehead Yeoman train.

**Saturday 17 May 1986**

*Above* The 'down side' of BR's modern image. The driver of No 73127, at the head of the Chipman's weedkilling train, peers from his cab looking for the green flag authorising him to proceed. The signal would not work, and by the look of Grain Crossing box - the victim of air-rifles or stones? - there will not be remedial attention for some time. . . *Brian Morrison*

**5 June 1986**

*Left* Originally built to serve St Pancras and the services to Bedford, Class '127' DMUs were ousted from this by the 'Bed-Pan' electric units, and some left the capital and were converted for parcels work in the North West by removing the seats and fitting roller shutter doors. These latter can clearly be seen in unit 916, comprising Nos 55976 (ex-51625) and 55986 (ex-51627) re-liveried into dark blue with red stripe, as it undertakes a Manchester-Preston service between Bolton and Lostock Junction. *Tom Heavyside*

**28 June 1986**
*Above left* From whichever way you look at it, York station is a magnificent structure, with the curved-arch train shed probably the best in the country. Unfortunately the overhead wires of electrification have not added to the appeal and for the best views we have to look back. In happier times, when loco-hauled trains were still very much in evidence, especially on cross-country duties, No 45040 has just arrived with a Liverpool-Scarborough train. The '45' will come off here, to give way to No 47488 waiting in the middle road. *Tom Heavyside*

**1 July 1986**
*Left* Back at the departure point of that cross-country train, there is another overall roof, although not as grand. No 31440 backs the stock that will form the 12.45 to Sheffield into Liverpool Lime Street station. Built in 1960 by Brush as D5628, the loco became 31440 in April 1984, after TOPS number 31204 had been worn since March 1974. Although looking in good condition at Liverpool, it was not to last much longer, being withdrawn from Immingham on 5 March 1987 and cut up by Vic Berry's yard in Leicester one year later. *Tom Heavyside*

**11 October 1986**
*Above* One thing that our railway heritage has given us is a bewildering variety of station layouts and architecture, much of it dictated of course by the position 'on the ground', as well as railway politics. Unfortunately too much has been swept away, some in the name of progress, but even in the 'eighties it was still possible to see character. This particular layout, at Ulverston, on the ex-Furness Railway route from Barrow to Carnforth, was highly unusual, but makes for a delightful picture as '108' DMU No 54262 leads sister 53955 into the station, forming the 13.45 Lancaster-Carlisle train (despite the destination blind!). *Tom Heavyside*

**6 November 1986**

South Wales has seen as much transformation in its railways as anywhere in the country, with the valleys being particularly hit; but much of that change, and the position both before and after, has been missed by railway photographers. Those who have visited to record, however, have come away with interesting and often poignant views. Treherbert used to be at the head of valley lines spreading south-west, south-east and north-east to Aberdare through a long tunnel. It lost the latter completely in 1966 and the south-west route to Bridgend to passengers on 15 July 1970, and the link completely in December of that year, but clung on to the ex-Taff Vale route to Cardiff and beyond, partly as single track. That stretch is seen here, near Ystrad Rhondda, as W51132 of Cardiff DMU set C331 leads a Treherbert-Penarth train. *Tom Heavyside*

*6 November 1986*
It would be interesting to know the history of the hill in the background and its fascinating folds. The shadows of the early afternoon sun make a very attractive backdrop to DMU set C304 as it arrives at Ton Pentre station, on the ex-Taff Vale Railway, as the reverse service, the 13.50 Penarth–Treherbert. Six weeks earlier, on 29 September, the station had been renamed from Ystrad Rhondda in preparation for the introduction of a timetabled half-hourly service, but the obvious track rationalisation and architectural rebuilding has destroyed the station's inherent aesthetic potential. *Tom Heavyside*

8 November 1986
Once again, an example of creating a pleasing picture by use of available 'material'. Another view of the Cardiff-Portsmouth service pre-'Sprinterisation', this time graced by No 33027 *Earl Mountbatten of Burma*, passing Bathampton. *Tom Heavyside*

**18 February 1987**
The introduction of the Class '59s' at the end of the decade truly transformed the Foster Yeoman stone trains, with their ability to haul prodigious loads unassisted pleasing their owners and amazing many within and without BR. Prior to their introduction double-heading was common, and here Nos 37001 (second-oldest of the class and adorned with Stratford's 'Cockney Sparrow' motif) and sister 37040 head up from Acton Poplar Junction to Acton Wells as the 09.05 Acton-Purfleet. *Colin Marsden*

**10 March 1987**
In the mid-'eighties some '45s' were fitted with a headlight, with a view to their being retained into the 'nineties. This policy was short-lived, however, and hardly had the fitting begun than the Class was facing extinction. One of the last 'first link' duties undertaken was on the Trans-Pennine route, linking the North East and North West. No 45137 (ex-*The Bedfordshire and Hertfordshire Regiment (TA)* but now without nameplates), although looking healthy enough accelerating out of Manchester Victoria at the head of the 08.20 Newcastle-Liverpool service, soon succumbed, being withdrawn from Tinsley on 15 June.

**10 March 1987**
*Left* On the same day, Class '25' No 25191 has even less time to live. Despite again looking in good shape and being usefully employed on a trip working through Manchester Victoria, she has but eight days left before being switched off with those of her sisters then still extant; then the 'Rats' were no more on BR.

**12 March 1987**
*Below left* Nottingham Midland station has seen many changes over the years and a few shifts of favour, with the varying fortunes of the Midland Main Line and the 'branch' through Trowell Junction. However, despite demographic changes it has retained a through service to London, and ended up optimistically at the end of the decade with the Trowell route saved, plans for re-opening services to Mansfield and rumours of some form of electrification. HST power car No 43122 waits to act as trailer car on the 11.50 train to St Pancras.

**12 March 1987**
*Below* 'Choppers' have been a part of the scene in the Midlands for the whole of their thirty-year career, usually coupled in pairs for freight and coal traffic and the occasional sortie to the seaside, but the writing was on the wall for them by the end of the decade, with changing freight patterns and the introduction of the Class '60s'. Nos 20190 and 20090, however, still have a few years left yet as their driver phones for instructions at Nottingham.

*19 April 1987*
The seafront railway at Dawlish is a scene that has remained relatively unchanged for the whole of this century and has been known and loved by countless millions of holiday-makers, but the motive power using it has changed greatly, some more quickly than others. 'Pacer' units (known as 'Skippers' in Devon and Cornwall) did not survive long in the South West, as their tyre wear was excessive compared to conventional DMUs. During its stay set 142025 heads away from Dawlish station as the 14.40 Exeter-Paignton. The spring sea is presumably too chilly for bathing! *Colin Marsden*

*21 April 1987*
A zoom lens can be a real asset for railway photography, giving an interesting slant with the slightly 'distorted' view. One is used here to advantage, together with the nerve to look into the sun, to place 'Pacer' 142023 amid the junction of lines at Aller Junction, forming an empty coaching stock train from Paignton to Exeter. *Colin Marsden*

*23 April 1987*
One of the delights of having your camera ever ready to record the scene wherever you happen to be is that you can capture views that will soon change, even when you are not aware of that impending change. Only months after I escaped from a ten-pin bowling match to snap No 7347, in Network SouthEast livery, as the trailing unit on the 15.06 Portsmouth Harbour-Waterloo, the deteriorating wooden canopy at Portsmouth & Southsea station, seen above the train and to the right, was swept away, to be replaced by a more modern affair.

*20 May 1987*
Another glimpse prior to change. Just a few months after this shot was taken, the 'Severn-Solent' service, from Portsmouth to Cardiff with a change of motive power at Bristol, was handed over to 'Sprinters'. Whilst obviating the need for lengthy negotiations at Bristol, the two-car units were no real replacement for a loco and several coaches. Here at Bristol Temple Meads the driver of No 33207 does not look happy about something - his past or his future? - as he leaves his charge, having backed it onto the stock that will become the 13.05 leg to Portsmouth Harbour.

*27 April 1987*
As mentioned earlier, Severn Tunnel Junction has seen its status greatly reduced, to the extent that the yards were taken out of use at the close of the decade, and Speedlink was withdrawn by Railfreight Distribution on 8 July 1991, forced to take the decision by Government profit constraints. Trains such as the 16.05 Eastleigh-Severn Tunnel Junction Speedlink service, seen passing through the Wylye Valley at Little Langford behind No 47142, therefore passed into history. Fortunately for enthusiasts and BR alike, not all the business was lost. *Brian Morrison*

*20 May 1987*
At platform 5 of Bristol Temple Meads, No 37429 *Sir Dyfed/County of Dyfed* starts the 12.50 service to Swansea. No 37429 had received the nameplates from No 37180 on 2 April, but then lost them again on 4 August 1987, to become *Eisteddfod Genedlaethol!*

**20 May 1987**
Swindon Works in its death throes. Contrary to local wishes or opinion, and to the disgust and outrage of railway-lovers everywhere, the decision was taken (some say with indecent haste) to close the historic cradle of the Great Western Railway. Fortunately not all was to be demolished, including the shops seen here, but the place will never be the same again. The final batch of locos at the Works was sold to Vic Berry for scrapping and is seen lined up ready for movement, with Nos 25027 and 25075 at the head of the queue. The trackwork here was severely rationalised shortly after this date.

**30 May 1987**
The shape of (some) things to come. With a reduction in rolling-stock requirements and a greater shift towards standardisation, wide variety will increasingly become a thing of the past. First-generation 'Sprinters' and EMUs shared a pedigree, and the ugly placing of corridor connections on the front-end is well evidenced here, as EMU unit No 5709 is well framed by the station structure leaving Clapham Junction as the 17.20 Waterloo-Dorking service. *Brian Morrison*

**3 July 1987**
The South East is a scene of regular services and constant bustle, and fortunately it seems that to date money has been spent on improving the services rather than sweeping away ancient infrastructure. There are still, therefore, delightful views such as this at Guildford, showing (left to right) '412/3' 4BEP No 2301 leading the 13.55 Waterloo–Portsmouth Harbour, '423' 4VEP No 7779 at the rear of the 14.30 Guildford–Waterloo, and '423' 4VEP No 7824 as the 'slow' 13.18 Waterloo–Portsmouth Harbour service.
*Brian Morrison*

**29 July 1987**
At the other end of the country the railway is vastly different, and you are more likely to find curlews than commuters! With some of the magnificent rugged Scottish scenery readily apparent, No 37413, now bearing the *Loch Eil Outward Bound* nameplates taken from No 37111, heads the 09.50 Glasgow-Fort William on the approach to Tyndrum Summit. From the mid-'eighties there has been wholesale restructuring of the '37s', with a great variety of amendments to enable them to fulfil specific duties as part of BR's shift towards 'Sectorisation'. No 37413, renumbered from 37276 in 1985, was one of the ETH programme for use in the Scottish Highlands. *Tom Heavyside*

**16 August 1987**
*Left* Birmingham Rail & Carriage Works turned out D5396 in June 1962, when it travelled south to be allocated to Cricklewood (14A). Most of its life, however, was spent in Scotland, where it became No 27108 under the TOPS system in April 1974, then 27052 ten years later. Withdrawn in early July 1987, one of the last of the Class to succumb, it was transferred back south with a number of Class relatives, to Vic Berry's yard. Initially this was to be for asbestos removal, as there was talk of preservation, but the loco failed to find a buyer and was eventually cut up at the Leicester site. In this in-between period it is seen at Vic Berry's yard looking remarkably healthy.

**22 August 1987**
*Below left* During the decade a number of routes were re-opened to steam. One which saw a number of trains was that from Gloucester to Swindon, although the occasions were much less frequent than, say, the S&C, the Cumbrian Coast or Marylebone-Stratford. It was therefore a real bonus when No 6201 *Princess Elizabeth* joined an elite band of locos to run the line, and despite the weather closing in after a glorious day, she still commands excited interest during a stop at Kemble.

**31 August 1987**
*Below* Introduced in 1981, the two '210' units were more experimental than anything else and were rarely seen on ordinary service trains. The second of the two, No 210 002, is therefore a welcome sight, as the only one then extant, drawing to a halt at Newbury on this bright sunny afternoon. Although not particularly successful in themselves, they did lend their experience to the design of others, such as the '317' EMUs.

*31 August 1987*
Once so much part of the scene out of Waterloo, on the Salisbury/Exeter trains, this once everyday scene became harder to find towards the close of the decade. Seen through a telephoto lens near Vauxhall, No 50008 *Thunderer* accelerates out of Waterloo with the 12.10 to Exeter St Davids, overtaking '455/7' No 5732 leading the 12.06 Waterloo-Chessington. *Brian Morrison*

*7 September 1987*
A week later *Thunderer* is seen again, but this time on ex-GWR metals, passing Old Oak Common with the 16.12 Paddington-Oxford. No 50002 *Superb* travels in the opposite direction, bringing empty coaching stock towards Paddington for use in a later service. Note how much more powerful *Thunderer* looks in large logo livery in this and the previous photograph, as opposed to the NSE livery worn by *Superb*. *Brian Morrison*

*18 September 1987*
Surely one of *the* most photographed trains of the whole decade, not least because of its double-heading by dedicated Class '37/5s', was the Lackenby-Corby Steel-liner service. Nos 37518 (ex-37076) and 37514 (37115) round the curve at Clay Cross Junction with a return working for Lackenby. *Colin Marsden*

*26 September 1987*
And surely one of the most celebrated sights was the infamous Vic Berry pile. At its height (if you will excuse the pun) there were around forty loco bodies stacked up, mostly Classes '25' and '27'. The bogies were separated for return to BR for re-use before the body shells were dealt with and any recoverable items retrieved or asbestos removed. Here the mobile crane adds to the general activity as Nos 25285, 25042 and 25089 await their fate with their sisters. These three had all been cut within a month, but several nearer the pile centre lasted much longer.

# 1988-1989

*18 April 1988*
Not only has Brian Morrison captured some of the variety of environments surrounding London's railways, and has used them well, but he has also captured here near Dartford three distinct styles of SR EMU numbering and livery. From left to right they are: a '415/1' 4EPB in blue/grey at the rear of the 16.37 Holborn Viaduct-Dartford via Bexleyheath, with the number centrally above the route indicator panel; '411/5' 4CEP No 1566 forming a Victoria-Sidcup-Dover Priory service, which has the number above each cab window and is in beige/brown 'jaffa cake' livery; and newly refurbished '423' 4CEP No 3194 in NSE livery and leading the 17.00 Gillingham-Cannon Street via Woolwich Arsenal, looking rather bare with the one number just visible below the grab rail beneath the driver's cab window.
*Brian Morrison*

**20 April 1988**
Who said there was no interest for steam buffs in modern railways! Trying its hardest to be a steam engine, judging by appearances, No 37232 seems to be overdoing the acceleration into Oxford station on a trip working. Anonymous at the time, No 37232 was named *The Institution of Railway Signal Engineers* (a name previously borne by No 37411) at BRML Springburn in November 1990, when allocated to Eastfield depot, and repainted in the then new 'Dutch' Departmental livery.

**21 May 1988**
It seems that, as built by the original railways, virtually every signal box was unique with its own constructional peculiarities. Snodland, on the ex-SE&CR Maidstone-Rochester branch, was no exception. The extension was originally built as a sort of corridor to give some protection to the keeper as he moved to the manual level-crossing; with the crossing now operated from within the box, the extension makes for an excellent greenhouse! Approaching it, '416/4' 2EPB No 6404 forms the 14.44 Maidstone West-Strood service. *Brian Morrison*

**31 May 1988**
When the Glanrhyd bridge on the Heart of Wales line was swept away in the autumn floods of 19 October 1987, Llandovery became the temporary southern rail terminus for the line from the north, the connections to Llandeilo being made by bus. DMU C853 (with W51808 leading) waits at Llandovery for the bus to arrive from Swansea, and will then form the 19.21 service to Crewe. In the early weeks/months after the accident, the line's support body, the Heart of Wales Line Travellers Association (HOWLTA) were fearful that the accident could be the death knell, but BR have been true to their promise that 'the line will not be closed. The bridge will be repaired.'

**13 June 1988**
By the end of the decade Class '33s' were increasingly being displaced from their normal routine duties, and sights such as this became rarer. No 33115 stands in Platform 3 at Salisbury coupled to Class '438' 4TC No 8017, waiting to form the 17.29 to Waterloo. At this time No 33115 was a humdrum member of the Class, but by the beginning of 1990, having been withdrawn from capital stock in May 1989, the loco achieved some notoriety, being converted at RFS Engineering in Doncaster for speed current collection trials in connection with proposed Channel Tunnel locomotives, and was based at Stewarts Lane depot. Unpowered, the loco retained its engine as ballast, was fitted with 750-volt DC shoegear for power transfer to specially converted No 73205, and was renumbered 83301.

*9 August 1988*

When Chris Green moved south from Scotland to become boss of Network SouthEast, one of his first moves was to inaugurate a corporate identity for the division. The NSE livery burst onto the scene as a colourful transformation of both rolling-stock and stations, to much comment, mostly complimentary, from both enthusiast and traveller alike. The initial design went through a couple of minor adjustments, but five years on was still the order of the day. Even in black and white, DMU L409 (with coach No 51344 nearest the camera) looks far more attractive than in the old blue and grey, as it stands at Pangbourne with the 17.41 Oxford-Paddington local service.

*16 August 1988*

Such has been the success of many railway services throughout the country, that extra trains are continually having to be found, totally confounding the doom brigade of the early 'eighties. One such extra, the 18.07 Paddington-Swindon, introduced in May and later extended to Bristol to meet local demands, brought booked loco-hauled passenger trains back to Swindon for the first time for many years. No 47551 heads the train into the lengthening sun, past the site of Uffington station.

*10 September 1988*
There are many anomalies on Britain's railways, not least the running of Network SouthEast to Exeter by way of the ex-LSWR route via Salisbury - not exactly the East! Still clinging on to the rostering, although threatened by rumours of replacement by Class '47's', No 50048 *Dauntless* winds out of Waterloo with the 11.10 to Exeter St Davids, with one blue and grey coach somewhat spoiling the otherwise all-NSE scene. *Brian Morrison*

*14 September 1988*

Many of the first-generation WCML electrics did not survive to the closing years of the decade, but a handful were retained for carriage shunting duties at Euston. Having been through the carriage washing plant regularly each day, No 83009 is almost white and looking a sorry sight at the buffer stops at Euston. Having been built as E3032 and released from Vulcan Foundry in November 1960, it suffered problems with the mercury arc rectifier along with its sisters and was placed in store between 1968 and 1971, pending refurbishment at Doncaster Works. Prior to transfer to Euston, No 83009 had spent two years as a mobile transformer at Longsight depot, and it lasted just six months after this shot, being withdrawn on 19 March 1989.

*1 October 1988*

The mid-Wales line to Aberystwyth enjoyed seesawing fortunes for many years, but ended the decade with a commitment to retention of services and a hope for the through trains to London. One such, and still loco-hauled at this stage, by engines unusual on London-bound trains elsewhere in the country, the 10.10 Aberystwyth-Euston is seen approaching Sutton Bridge Junction, Shrewsbury, behind Nos 37680 (refurbished in April 1987 from No 37224) and 37684 (from 37134 in March 1987). *Tom Heavyside*

**9 October 1988**
*Below* One of the definite highlights of the year was the first Bescot Open Day, albeit with dismal or very wet weather, depending on the time of day. Early on in the events, refurbished and re-classified to Standard Class only for the Provincial Sector, and re-liveried in appropriate sector livery, re-numbered No 310 101 (ex-310 073) stands lined up for inspection at the head of the yard display.

**30 October 1988**
*Right* In the early hours of 28 October, Nos 31202 and 31226 overran buffer stops at speed at Brent Sidings, Cricklewood, ending up on the North Circular Road with the latter on top of the former! Immediately condemned on site, Vic Berry's men were dispatched to take No 31202 back to Leicester, where it arrived in two sections on the morning of the 30th. Later that day it is seen awaiting the cutter's torch. Introduced, to Ipswich (32B), in June 1960 as D5626, but a resident of Finsbury Park shed for many years, it was renumbered under TOPS in February 1974, and was allocated to Stratford at the time of the accident.

**30 October 1988**
*Below right* As well as cutting locos and handling asbestos removal, Vic Berry also undertook repainting for both BR and LUT, winning an enviable reputation for the quality of the finished product. Obviously needing clean conditions, the paint sheds were not the most comfortable places to work in, as can be seen from this shot of No 31130, masked and in yellow undercoat. One of the Crewe nuclear flask pool, No 31130 was the second of this sub-Sector to be dealt with by Vic Berry, following No 31275, which had been completed in the new Railfreight livery earlier in the month.

*23 November 1988*
*Left*  The development of Sectorisation on BR meant that all manner of operating areas were 'owned' by various Sectors of the organisation. This even extended to particular services, with the North East-South West sub-Sector of InterCity supervising the 15.28 Poole-Liverpool train, seen here at Oxford behind No 47663. The engine has not been long in this guise, having been transferred to this number (from 47240) under the ETH conversion programme in January 1987, only to be renumbered again in February 1989 to 47818, with the fitting of long-range fuel tanks.

*23 November 1988*
*Below left*  The introduction of 'Sprinters' was to be the answer to many prayers, but they were not without their problems. Class '155s' especially caused serious headaches, by having door problems shortly after integration into rosters, and the whole Class was temporarily withdrawn from service on Friday 16 December 1988. Set 155308, only days away from this and the necessary remedial action, is seen standing in Platform 3 of Oxford station, shortly before becoming the 20.18 Oxford-Worcester train.

*28 November 1988*
*Below*  The 'East Coast Revival', the electrification of the ECML, cost £517 million - the largest single investment on BR for some considerable time - and reached completion from London to Edinburgh in the summer of 1991. The route to Leeds, however, was energised from October 1988 and much play was made of the launch of the InterCity 225s, 'Electras', from GEC for this. They were to be the flagship of the line, bringing to the capital main-line 'push-pull' working, with attendant Class '82' DVTs, and were definitely considered the way to the future. On a driver training special, No 91008 really looks the part (despite the old-liveried stock behind it!), waiting to leave King's Cross to take the road to Peterborough. *Colin Marsden*

*7 December 1988*
Despite much electrification and re-signalling throughout the country, there were pockets where old practices died hard. Apart from the loco, this view is timeless, with a ballast train, semaphore signals and a railman attending to the lamps of the signals, oilcan in hand. In 'GW150' green and brass cabside numbers, applied for the 1985 celebrations, No 47628 *Sir Daniel Gooch* approaches High Wycombe with an up works ballast train.

**11 December 1988**
With the re-routing of various InterCity services between London and Birmingham, Coventry gained an increased importance and a thorough mix of motive power. On the left, NSE-liveried No 47582 *County of Norfolk* pauses with the 08.40 Paddington-Wolverhampton, whilst on the right No 86103 *André Chapelon* passes with a Euston-Preston train.

**9 February 1989**
To partly replace D200, when it was withdrawn, the original Class '37', D6700, was repainted in near-original green livery at Crewe in February/March 1988, when it became the last of the Class to receive an intermediate overhaul at the Works. Initially carrying both D6700 and 37119 (its TOPS number), it was renumbered to D6700/37350 by the end of March as part of the fitting of regeared CP7 bogies, working from Cardiff Canton shed, usually on Ripple Lane petroleum diagrams. An alternative working was the 11.20 Theale-Robeston oil train turn, usually double-headed, and this is seen passing the site of Challow station with 'Green Goddess II' coupled behind No 37371 in old-style Railfreight livery. One of the appeals of railway photography for me, as true now as in steam days, is the possibility of something 'turning up' that you were not expecting, and this is an example of just such an event.

*17 February 1989*
As if to prove that attractive photographs are possible in less than ideal conditions, and that you should never put your camera away, the photographer has made excellent use of rain, lights and a slow shutter to capture No 43074 dramatically powering up at King's Cross, on a down express. Surrounding it and awaiting their rights of way for the north are, left to right, Nos 89001 *Avocet*, 43197 and 43121 (ex-*West Yorkshire Metropolitan County*). *Colin Marsden*

**14 March 1989**
By the end of the 'eighties, plans were well advanced for a series of 'light' railways in and around Manchester, part of which would affect the terminal platforms at Manchester Victoria. As if blissfully unaware of the fate awaiting it, the station gives temporary refuge to 'Pacer' unit No 142051 (55701 leading), waiting to form the 11.10 service to Rochdale via Oldham. By the look on the ganger's face, perhaps he has heard of the plans and fears for his job!

**14 March 1989**
In those same suburban platforms at Manchester Victoria, a prospective passenger prepares to stow his bike aboard Class '504' Manchester-Bury dc EMU No M65457, in Metro orange livery, which will leave as the 11.44 service to Bury. When the LRT was developed in 1991/2, these platforms were swept away and the units were assigned to the scrap-heap, with just a few exceptions.

*14 March 1989*
As in the King's Cross photograph (page 136), rain has been used to enhance the view, with the reflections adding to this portrait of EMU set 304 005 as it enters Platform 13 of Manchester Piccadilly with the 12.30 service to Crewe. A perfectly ordinary scene at the time, all but four of the Class '304' units were withdrawn twelve months later, and many went to and were cut up at Vic Berry's Leicester yard very shortly after.

*14 March 1989*
Of all the many variations of livery that BR perpetrated during the 'eighties, none was more irritating for both enthusiast and railmen alike, causing complaints from both, than the InterCity version with microscopic loco numbers. Even at close range, standing still at the buffers at Manchester Piccadilly, it is not easy to read No 87005 *City of London*'s identification. Thankfully some sense did surface, with larger numbers again appearing, but this merely added to the ever-widening variety of livery styles!

**23 March 1989**
With the continued non-availability of 'Sprinters', short loco-hauled formations became an increasingly common sight in the closing years of the decade. No 50005 *Collingwood* is most definitely not over-worked handling just two Mark 1 BSKs, and attracting very little other than the photographer's attention, leaving Dawlish with the 10.50 Paignton-Cardiff. *Colin Marsden*

**26 March 1989**

*Left* An increasingly rare sight as the years wore on was '20s' on a mixed freight. Despite the time of year, the sun is hot and high, making one feel lethargic, a feeling echoed in the easy pace of Nos 20157 and 20007 as they amble through Leicester (London Road) station with a northbound train.

**26 March 1989**

*Below* On the same day, Leicester depot yard was home to a surprisingly varied line-up. From left to right are Nos 31185, 47320, 56061, 46023 (alias Departmental No 97402) and DMU L101 (alias Old Oak-allocated route-learning car Departmental TDB975023, and ex-W55001). With the latter two already withdrawn from even Departmental service, and with a never-ending push towards greater standardisation, views such as this became ever rarer in the later years of the decade and beyond.

**30 March 1989**

*Above right* First-generation DMUs became ever more attractive and photographically sought after as their numbers dwindled. With withdrawals and accident damage, there were many reformations of sets and it was often difficult to keep pace with developments. Remarkably stable at this time, however, was the spare Reading set L842 (comprising Nos 53314, nearest the camera, 59101 and 53327); this set achieved some notoriety on 19 November 1988 when it was despatched to work the Ashford-Hastings services in place of DEMU No 205018, which had suffered a traction motor failure, but failed itself at Staplehurst! Repaired and back on its home ground, the set has a misleading destination blind, being the 17.41 *from* Oxford, bound for Reading, and preparing to leave Pangbourne.

**13 April 1989**

*Below* One of the most successful innovations of recent years has been the Thameslink service, running through trains from Brighton to Bedford across the Thames. One of the very attractive '319' sets, No 319 056, of the type handling the service, departs from Clapham Junction with the 16.40 Victoria-Brighton, a train this time staying south of the river. Design ideas changed through the decade with, thankfully, aesthetics being brought into consideration with the later editions of rolling-stock, and hideous corridor ends becoming more a thing of the past. *Colin Marsden*

*21 May 1989*
It used to be just steam excursions that drew the crowds, but with an increasing population that never knew 'real' steam, modern traction has become ever more popular, with a resultant increase in railtours thus hauled. A delightful innovation and a highlight of 1989 was the InterCity Diesel Day, organised by Hertfordshire Railtours, where a variety of trains were run between Leicester and St Pancras, hauled by most unusual motive power. This was much appreciated by enthusiasts, as was the weather by photographers! The day was hot and sunny and some of the heat haze can be seen behind No 37058 as it heads north under the wires past Sundon, north of Luton, with the 10.40 ex-St Pancras.

**1 June 1989**
Another innovation, following in the tradition set by the 'GW150' celebrations, was the painting of Class '47' No 97561 in Midland Railway maroon and its naming, on 23 May 1989, as *Midland Counties Railway 150 1839-1989* to celebrate the 150th Anniversary of the 'birth' of the Midland Railway. The engine was used by Derby Control on a number of specials over the next few weeks, and a mere nine days later, and still looking magnificent in this livery, it stands at Hellifield station, having brought a BR special from Leicester. Interestingly, the loco was only in this guise for a very short period, as the BR computer could not cope with this number and it was re-numbered 47973 on 15 July, and then re-painted and de-named in March 1990! To the right, preserved '8F' No 48151 can be seen waiting to take over the train to Carlisle.

**1 June 1989**
Having taken over the train, the Stanier '8F' took it to Carlisle, where it then retired to Upperby depot for attention, whilst the travellers amused themselves around the town. Having had its smokebox emptied, and coal and water replenished, the loco prepares to run back to Citadel station, looking very much at home on shed and evoking fond memories of steam days.

**1 June 1989**
The problems with the introduction of 'Sprinters' - the door problems and the late introduction of later builds - led to loco-plus-coach substitution on an ever-widening, although somewhat temporary, basis. At Carlisle the 14.05 ex-Newcastle is the focus of attention, as it arrives at its destination, 8 minutes late, behind No 47501 *Craftsman* in place of a 'Sprinter'.

**1 June 1989**
Livery permutations literally ran riot by the end of the decade, and all manner of variations cropped up, with many nostalgically harking back to the early days of dieselisation. Painted in green, with front whiskers and mid-period BR totem on the carriage side, DMU set CH274 (comprising Class '108' Nos E54247 and 53964) stands in Carlisle station waiting to form the 18.30 service to Barrow.

**2 June 1989**
Compare this view with that on page 42 and see how much has disappeared. Fortunately the ARC yard at Loughborough still sees healthy freight traffic, and here No 56050 is backing into the yard with a rake of empties. The view now, however, looks bare and devoid of the interest that the old warehouse and signal box gave; happily, the Brush Works on the extreme left is still thriving, and at least the remaining station architecture has received a welcome coat of paint.

**2 June 1989**
One more step towards standardisation was the removal of the ex-MR lamps from Leicester depot yard in 1989, to be replaced by a small number of huge tower structures. As can be seen, the engineers' preparations are well advanced, and the crop of railway 'bullrushes' surrounding No 31102 will soon be a thing of the past.

*10 June 1989*
Another view of the stupid small-number InterCity livery; fortunately the bridge latticework and trolley silhouette counterbalance the visual interest as No 47568 prepares to leave Cheltenham with the 08.20 Tenby-York 'InterCity Holiday-maker' service, carrying holidaymakers back home.

*10 June 1989*
Holiday specials have long brought unusual workings and 1989 was no exception, with some North West-Devon/Cornwall trains being rostered for double-headed '31s'. Nos 31421 (in Corporate Blue) and 31455 (in brand new Departmental grey, and to be re-numbered 31555 one year later) accelerate south through Cheltenham with the 09.18 Manchester-Paignton, eliciting no response from a lone commuter! Having just 'dropped in' to the station during a shopping trip, this was another of those surprise bonuses.

**15 June 1989**
Another lesson in how to make a picture of SR EMUs interesting. The tell-tale chimneys of Battersea Power Station give the game away for the area, and the London architecture and foliage add to the view of, on the left, '416/3' 2EPB No 6314 making the prescribed stop at Wandsworth Road station with the 18.21 London Bridge-Victoria service. In the centre '415/4' 4EPB No 5459 heads towards Factory Junction, Battersea, with the 18.19 Orpington-Victoria, whilst on the right '415/1' and '415/6' 4EPBs Nos 5248 and 5601 'double-head' the 18.32 Victoria-Orpington away from the metropolis. *Brian Morrison*

*24 June 1989*
Once again Brian Morrison shows why he is a successful professional transport photographer, delightfully framing '411/5' 4CEP No 1578 and '423/0' 4VEP No 3163 jointly forming the 18.09 Dover Priory-Victoria service at Canterbury East. The semaphore helps to make the picture, but pride of place goes to the elevated ex-SE&CR box; one wonders whether the signalman was paid danger money for those stairs! *Brian Morrison*

**25 June 1989**
Such was the success of the four initial Class '59s' that a fifth was ordered from General Motors by Foster Yeoman. Not long after its arrival, No 5 stands in the centre of the group, specially arranged for the photograph, at Merehead, after being shown off during an Open Day. From left to right they are Nos 59001 *Yeoman Endeavor*, 59002 *Yeoman Enterprise*, 59005 *Kenneth J. Painter*, 59003 *Yeoman Highlander*, and 59004 *Yeoman Challenger*. Somewhat surprisingly, the fifth member did not carry on the naming tradition of its predecessors, but was named at the Open Day by Mr Painter himself, a member of the Foster Yeoman management team, to his own complete surprise! *Colin Marsden*

**8 July 1989**
This weekend saw the Centenary of the railway coming to Chesham, and to celebrate the event the Saturday and Sunday and the weekend before saw special shuttles from Chesham to Watford, with steam one end and preserved Metropolitan electric No 12 *Sarah Siddons* at the other, causing a great stir locally, as steam was last seen on these third-rail lines over 25 years previously. The steam loco was Metropolitan No 1, normally kept at Quainton Road, and she is the distinct focus of attention as she accelerates round the bend into Rickmansworth station with the 12.20 ex-Watford return; London Underground battery loco No 18 is being totally ignored in the bay platform.

**31 July 1989**
The Central Wales line to Aberystwyth and Porthmadog is one of great scenic beauty, but for railway fans possesses little variety. Freights are distinct highlights, therefore, especially so when headed by the ever-popular Class '37s'. No 37426 *Y Lein Fach/Vale of Rheidol* - somewhat appropriately named - makes a fine sight, despite the dull weather, entering Machynlleth station on an oil train from Aberystwyth.

**12 August 1989**
Another of the year's centenaries was that of the Brush Engineering Works in Loughborough. To celebrate, the company resurrected a past tradition of Open Days and the day was graced by a visit from a descendant of the founding US family. For rail fans, however, the definite centre of interest was the new build of Class '60s', and inside the finishing shop were, left to right, Nos 60006, 60003, 60005 and 60007. The bodies were built and basically painted by Procor in Rotherham, after which they were shipped by road to Loughborough, for Brush to complete the fitting out and handing over to BR.

*12 August 1989*

A visit to Vic Berry's scrapyard in Leicester was always one of anticipation and often one of surprise. I visited the site on numerous occasions, and always with the same results - there was sadness at the sight of locos being laid to their final rest, often without any ceremony, but I was always keyed up by what might be just around the corner. Over the years Vic Berry cut, de-asbestosed or renovated almost every class of engine withdrawn during the decade, often with the sadness quotient very high among enthusiasts, not least when it came to the '50s'. It was heartbreaking to see the once mighty machines in such a state as No 50012 *Benbow*, seen here with its back broken, having been withdrawn from Laira in January. I was doubly sorry to see this loco in such a state, as I had enjoyed its haulage of a special from High Wycombe to Derby three years earlier, via the freight-only Knighton Junction-Burton-on-Trent line, ironically passing the approaches to the Vic Berry yard!

*12 August 1989*

And just to prove that nothing is permanent or enjoys a divine right, even 'Sprinters' could be scrapped so soon after being introduced. Coach No 52212, one of a pair damaged beyond economical repair in a collision at Seamer, south of Scarborough on the ex-NER route to York (the other was 52209), and now covered in 'artistic' graffiti, rests on trestles at Vic Berry's yard, stripped of bogies and other salvageable parts and awaiting the cutter's torch. Ironically, the much older steam saddle-tank was awaiting renovation!

*5 September 1989*
Such has been the change in BR's operations during the 'eighties that almost anything can happen. Once fully employed on the Glasgow-Edinburgh push-pulls, and unlikely to roam far, the specially fitted '47/7s' became threatened by the introduction of Class '158' 'Express' units and were destined to move to the other end of the country. The problems with introduction of these units, however, meant that many of the '47s' received a reprieve. However, No 47714 did become surplus, the first to be so, was transferred south to Old Oak Common shed, was re-liveried for Network SouthEast, lost its *Grampian Region* nameplates, and was put to work on Paddington-Oxford services. Here it has just arrived with the 16.15 ex-Paddington. The idea was to oust Class '50s' from the route, but these, too, received a late stay of execution.

*6 September 1989*
With the splitting of BR into separate 'businesses', which would bid and quote for work, strange workings could be seen almost anywhere. One such, seen approaching the ex-GWR station site at Challow in bright sunshine, is DMU set L409, in NSE livery, returning empty coaching stock to Reading, having been to Cardiff Canton for wheel turning!

**5 October 1989**
A last look at Vic Berry's yard, a place which disappeared from the enthusiasts' itinerary in the early 1990s after a massive fire amongst the stock. Looking for all the world as if it could be running a local service, ex-Chester DMU set CH617 (with M53465 nearest) is merely waiting for that final fatal attention.

**23 October 1989**
It's amazing where ex-BR engines will turn up. Long withdrawn, but having received cosmetic restoration to pseudo-GWR livery, complete with cast cabside number, ex-'03' No (D)2022 was moved from the Swindon & Cricklade Railway on semi-permanent loan to Coopers (Metals) Ltd of Swindon, to replace that company's own failed shunter. With scrap metal obviously being prepared in the background, the engine ticks over on its holding siding, before moving forward to move the scrap wagons onto BR metals.

**24 October 1989**
*Left* As the decade ended, the HSTs built for the westbound route out of Paddington celebrated at least a decade of hard work. Logging up many hundreds of miles daily, they have been incredibly successful in taking BR forward and re-attracting travellers to the rails. Although far more mundane to watch than a loco and coaches, they have a definite aesthetic style, and some of this is demonstrated by power car No 43145 as it stands at Newport waiting to continue with the 12.00 Paddington-Swansea InterCity service and bearing the latest livery.

**24 October 1989**
*Below left* They may be life-expired, but South Wales, in common with other parts of the country, had to keep its first-generation DMUs going at all costs. Having already served for thirty years, DMU set B971 is about to set out from Newport, earning yet more revenue as the 12.47 service to Abergavenny, but with the doors still ready to accept passengers. With the onset of 'Sprinters' and 'SuperSprinters', and the imminent arrival of 'Express' and 'Turbo' units, it is unlikely that these elderly DMUs will see many more winters.

**6 December 1989**
*Above right* The shape of (some) things to come. With plans to build 200 fully air-conditioned Class '471' 'Networker Express' units to replace the entire existing Kent Coast fleet of ageing EMUs, a full-size mock-up was unveiled at Victoria station in London in the presence of Chris Green, Director of NSE, and Michael Portillo, Transport Minister, to gauge customer and staff reaction before the design was finalised. The impressive front end is dramatically captured by this shot. *Brian Morrison*

**14 October 1989**
*Below* Twilight for the decade and for many more loco classes. Superbly caught in car headlights, three classes that will undoubtedly be increasingly affected in the 1990s line up at March depot. Left to right, they are Nos 20186 (stored unserviceable at Toton two years later), 37711 *Tremorfa Steelworks* (renovated in 1988 from No 37085 and hopefully with a good few years left yet), and 31135, the ex-D5553 of 1959 and living on borrowed time? *Brian Morrison*

# CHRONOLOGY OF THE 1980s

## 1980

### January

First 'Deltics' withdrawn - Nos 55001 *St Paddy* and 55020 *Nimbus*. No 84009 converted to Mobile Load Bank. Reading-Gatwick Airport service introduced.

### February

APT restarts Euston-Glasgow tests. No 08934, BR's last green shunter, goes into Works for attention and repaint into blue. Dolgellau bypass started on site of ex-GW trackbed.

### March

New business on ECML HSTs causing overcrowding; four new sets ordered. St Erth-Acton milk train ended.
1-3 Gidea Park-Forest Gate Junction changed to 25kV.

### April

New BR trains on Kidderminster-Bewdley to link with SVR. Sign erected at King's Cross prohibiting 'locospotters'!
3 End of Class '27' on Glasgow-Edinburgh Push-Pull.

### May

Class '33s' take over Bristol-Portsmouth, and '50s' Waterloo-Exeter services. HSTs out of Paddington accelerated to give some 100 mph start-to-stop schedules.
24-26 Rainhill Cavalcade.

### June

End of Toton-Willesden freights - threat to Market Harborough-Northampton line. BREL 7 per cent cut-back in scheduled repairs. No 47901 finally leaves Crewe, for Cardiff/Margam.

### July

New Class '315' EMUs at Shenfield and Ilford for training. Threat to Barmouth Bridge from marine worms - local fears of closure.
10 Five bolts found at Rugby,

sheared off APT trailer car!

### August

'Jubilee' No 5690 *Leander* borrowed by BR off 'Cumbrian Mountain express' to help ailing Class '40'! Lifting of Stratford-upon-Avon to Cheltenham Lansdown Junction complete except for Honeybourne-Long Marston stretch.
3 Ryburgh-Fakenham closed (and lifted next day!).

### September

First set of ETH coach stock to Yarmouth for 'East Anglian'. No 50003 *Temeraire* becomes first of Class in new 'large logo' livery.
7 No 55003 *Meld* is first of Class to Blackpool.

### October

No 24081 withdrawn - last of Class. Class '502' EMUs withdrawn from Merseyside after 40 years.
12 Barmouth Bridge closed.
18 Hump shunting ends at Whitemoor yard.

### November

Classes '44' and '84' extinct in BR stock; No 84002 sold to GEC as generator.
1 'The Night Ferry' ceases. On first steam special over Settle-Carlisle No 46229 *Duchess of Hamilton* slips to a halt at Stainforth Tunnel!

### December

Class '315' EMUs start running out of Liverpool Street. New carriage washing plant in use at Southend.
5 Bury-Rawtenstall suddenly closed by BR.

## 1981

### January

No 05001 withdrawn, last of Class with others gone in 1966-68! Dronfield station re-opened, and new Barking platform at

Gospel Oak. Bedford-Luton Hoo energised.

### February

Report on Ribblehead Viaduct says it is in poor condition, possibly beyond repair! New DMU - No 140001 - on test Derby-Bedford.
20 98 withdrawn locos awaiting attention at Swindon Works!

### March

No 01002 withdrawn - last of Class.
2 Coach of 07.10 Marylebone-Aylesbury bursts into flames - totally gutted with intense heat, but no one hurt!
15 Colour lights on Caterham branch.

### April

Newport-Didcot coal trains ended, but Shotton-Llanwern re-started. Last '03s' transferred from Darlington.
25-26 Heavy snow puts Swindon-Gloucester signalling out.

### May

Last 'Deltics' transferred away from Finsbury Park. Barmouth Bridge re-opened. Gateshead turntable installed at Scarborough.
22 Honeybourne station re-opened.

### June

New coal terminal opened at Garston Dock.
1 Parcels trains withdrawn from Oxford station.
8 No 13002 withdrawn - sign of decline of Tinsley yard.

### July

1 Bricklayers Arms parcels (ex-goods) depot closed after 137 years.
18 Woodhead route closed and Class '76' therefore extinct - No 76054 is last of Class.
29 Prince and Princess of Wales start honeymoon, travel-

ling Waterloo-Romsey behind No 73142 *Broadlands*.

### August

No 40122 (D200) withdrawn.
16 Market Harborough-Northampton line closed.
17 Former Glasgow Class '304' EMUs start on Crewe-Liverpool turns.

### September

No 06002 withdrawn - last of Class.
11 Last scheduled service of Class '306' EMUs (Shenfield units).
28 Luton Hoo-Cricklewood energised.

### October

All Class '40s' in Scotland transferred south.
4 Newton Abbot stabling point and Wellingborough depots closed.
5 Wetherall station re-opened after 15 years, and Kentish Town West after 10 years.

### November

'Open Station' operation on Highland and Far North lines. Closure notices posted for Broad Street. Last Class '111' DMU buffet cars withdrawn.

### December

7 APT enters public service - short-lived!
9 HST to East Lancs line for Jimmy Savile 'Age of the Train' advert filming.
10 No 47406 named *Rail Riders* after BR young persons' club.

## 1982

### January

4 Last 'Deltics' withdrawn - Nos 55002, 55009, 55015, 55022 (ex-D9000). York loses allocation of locos except shunters.
13-8 February ASLEF rail dispute.

## February
Some fitted freight and Speedlink services diverted from S&C to WCML. Start made on repainting IoW '485/6' units.
1 Airdrie-Bathgate line closed.

## March
West Highland line now under 'one engine in steam' working.
14 Mallaig signal box closed.
22 New Blaenau Ffestiniog Central station opened, with *Blanche* on FR tracks alongside.

## April
2 Kensington Motorail terminal closed.
5 Last Class '315' EMU enters service.
26 New station at Deighton opened.

## May
'Scotrail' brand name introduced.
14 Milton Keynes Central station opened.
17 Watton-at-Stone re-opened, after 43 years! Nottingham-Glasgow and Leeds-Morecambe services diverted away from S&C.

## June
Aberystwyth signal box closed and station reduced to single platform working.
5 Forfar-Perth line closed.
28-29 NUR rail dispute.

## July
Vauxhall Motors switch Luton-Ellesmere Port car deliveries from rail to road.
3-19 Further ASLEF disputes; some freight contracts cancelled as a result.
12 150th Anniversary of Leicester-Swannington opening.

## August
Tracklifting on Three Spires Junction-Gosford Green branch, Coventry.
2 New Chapeltown station opened.
9 Danygraig wagon repair shops closed.

## September
No 58001 completed. DEMU sets 210001/2 enter service. First Class '56' - No 56046 - allocated to WR.
5 First passenger train at Templecombe since 1966.
27 St Pancras-Bedford ('Bed-Pan') route now fully 'live'.

## October
4 Ebbw Junction depot closed, and new Norwich Crown Point carriage depot opened.
17 £12m Southampton area re-signalling completed.
20 HM The Queen Mother names No 47541 *The Queen Mother* at Aberdeen.

## November
6 Barnstaple-Torrington closed.
16 New Class '455' EMU - No 5805 - on display at Waterloo.
29 March-Spalding line closed.

## December
6 BR tests with 66 PGAs and two Class '56s', Merehead-Southall.
9 Press launch for No 58001 (in new Railfreight livery), and last Class '56' built at Doncaster.
13 New station at Slaithwaite opened after 14 years.

## 1983

### January
Serpell Committee Report published - potentially as damaging as Beeching. Wath Depot closed.
8 Passenger services Glasgow-Kilmacolm withdrawn.
22 Clayton West branch closed.

### February
Tracklifting on Kilmacolm branch. Rail link to BNFL storage dump at Drigg completed.
11 Switch of container traffic at Dagenham Storage Ltd from road to rail.

### March
Training begins on driver-only-operated (DOO) trains, Bedford-St Pancras.
3 No 47469 named *Glasgow Chamber of Commerce* at Glasgow Queen St.

### April
BR agrees to restore No 40122 (D200) to working order - repaint paid for by *Rail Enthusiast* magazine.
18 'Bed-Pan' electrics now on some services.
26 First HST power car named - No 43113 *City of Newcastle*.

### May
Nos 82005/8 reinstated for ecs workings at Euston.
13 Elmers End-Sanderstead closed.
16 New third-rail Hunt Cross-Garston opened to passengers. Pinhoe station re-opened, the first under the 'Speller Amendment'.

### June
No 50014 *Warspite* in Doncaster Works - last '50' for refurbishment and 'large logo' livery.
15 King's Cross ceremony for first HST set to pass million-mile mark.
19 First HST to Aberystwyth.

### July
Announcement of plans to close Ribblehead-Appleby and Marylebone to Northolt Junction - fight to save both begins. No 83012 in use on ecs at Euston. Crewe Works starts fitting large fixed-beam headlights to Class '47s'.

### August
Nos 25305/314 at Derby for conversion to 'Ethels' (electric train heating) to join No 25310 already converted.
6 Pontardulais Tunnel re-opened after remedial work.

### September
New InterCity livery trialed on HST set No 253028. 'Manchester Pullman' cars re-painted in APT-style livery, and Strathclyde PTE livery applied to No 303008. Scotrail launches 'Go Anywhere' £5 day return campaign.

### October
Selby diversion line opened - first new of stretch main line this century. Last SR EMU Class '405' (4SUB) withdrawn.
3 New Cardiff Cathays station opened. Templecombe re-opened, and Coulsdon North closed.

### November
4 Cornish Railcard introduced.
20 Bodmin Parkway-Wenford Bridge closed.
21 Moss Side, near Lytham, re-opened after 22 years.

### December
Nos 302255/75 are first Class '302' EMUs withdrawn. No 37015 is first in new wrap-around yellow ends and 'large logo' livery.
31 Radipole station closed.

## 1984

### January
New Chairman for BR, but BREL announces large job losses. Class '25s' transferred away from London.
5 First on-train payphone launched on Paddington-Swansea HST.

### February
6 Press run for new Gatwick service.
13 WR headquarters move from Paddington to Swindon.
25 No 50007 repainted green and renamed *Sir Edward Elgar*.

### March
17 Consett line closed.
19 No 141006 in West Yorks PTE light green and cream livery. 23 Refurbished Haymarket station opened.
26 New Aberdeen-Wick container introduced.

### April
First section of conductor rail laid on Hastings line.
3 Class '114' DMU repainted in South Yorks PTE livery.
9 Saltaire station opened.
14 New Maidstone East panel commissioned and signal boxes on line to Ashford closed.

### May
'Bustitution' linking Peterborough with Kettering withdrawn - uneconomic! Bradford Hammerton Street and Darlington DMU depots closed.
13 End of Class '123/124' DMUs on Trans-Pennine services.
14 Lostock Hall station re-opened after 15 years.

### June
No 45003 is now last of Class with split-headcode boxes.
25 Abolition of ER Divisional management structure.
29 Shilton Wagon Works closed.
30 Abingdon branch closed.

### July
6 Pioneering Radio Electronic Token Block (RETB) signalling inaugurated at Dingwall.
17 CEGB stages crash at Old Dalby between No 46009 and nuclear flask at 100 mph!
23 New station at South Bank on Middlesbrough-Saltburn line.

### August
Ex-diesel loco shed at King's Cross demolished.
8 APT back on revenue-earning runs.
17 No 150001 on test, Derby-St Pancras.
30 No 43002 named *Top of the*

*Pops* on TV after record-breaking Paddington-Bristol run.

### September

18,000 objections so far against S&C closure!

**15** Dyce station opened.

**17** Lever Brothers promotion - free train ticket for three coupons from their products.

### October

'86s' on GE for driver training.

**1** Dunston station re-opened after 58 years (!) and Livingstone station opened. 'Starlight Express', Euston-Glasgow overnight service, launched and No 86242 named by Andrew Lloyd Webber.

### November

No 303060 painted in Manchester PTE brown and orange livery, and No 47708 in Scotrail livery.

**25** Last Class '46' is withdrawn.

**30** Tonbridge-Hastings line christened '1066 Route'.

### December

**8** Last of Class '506' 1,500-volt dc EMUs withdrawn.

**17** Tinsley hump closed.

**20** Summit Tunnel explosion and fire closes line.

## 1985

### January

Reading Signal Works closed. Track singled over Ribblehead Viaduct.

**21** Last Class '13' is withdrawn.

### February

Nos 47484 and 47628 in lined Brunswick green livery with brass numbers and names, ready for GW150 celebrations.

**2** Launch of 'Valley Lines' identity in South Wales.

**8** Class '151' DMU unveiled at Met-Cam in Birmingham.

### March

Wirral lines Class '503' EMUs withdrawn. No 47487 becomes first of Class in InterCity livery.

**17** New Eltham station opened.

### April

Brighton area signalling scheme completed six months early. No 37005 in Works as first conversion to freight-only No 37501, and No 37268 as ETH-fitted No 37401.

**15** Outward Bound Lochiel station opened.

### May

'Manchester Pullman' coaches withdrawn. Marylebone services given 'Chiltern Line' identity.

**11** Lincoln St Marks closed.

**17** Class '142' railbus unveiled.

### June

**1** Reading hosts first of six Open Days on WR for GW150 celebrations.

**2** Crewe station closed for seven weeks for re-modelling; four Class '40s' reprieved to assist.

### July

**6** Eridge-Tunbridge Wells West closed.

**15** Travellers Fare introduce modular catering service.

**29** Didcot Parkway opens.

### August

No 143001 on BR for testing. Transport Police Q-trains introduced into South Wales.

**14** Castleton, Rochdale, railmaking depot opened.

### September

Three '501' units converted for Sandite use on Merseyside.

**26** Renovated Watford Junction station opened.

**30** Rock Ferry-Hooton electric service introduced. Class '142' 'Pacers' in service. Dufftown branch closed.

### October

No 03170 last of Class overhauled at Swindon. Class '150/1' introduced for testing.

**17** Adderley Park and Marston Green stations, Birmingham, opened.

### November

**4** Lisvane & Thornhill station opened.

**8** Sir Stanley Matthews names new 'Manchester Pullman' coach after himself.

**11** First '25/9' created (ex-25283) for minerals and chemicals sectors.

### December

No 08675 becomes final '08' repaired at Swindon.

**16** New travel centre at Inverness; RETB to Wick and Thurso 'opened', and No 37417 named *Highland Region*.

## 1986

### January

**3** New Oban station opened.

**16** Start of Petfoods Speedlink trains from Melton Mowbray.

**21** Class '59s' arrive at Southampton from Chicago.

### February

Conductor rails installed, Sanderstead-East Grinstead.

**5** 'Sprinters' press launch in East Anglia.

**8** 'Sprinters' introduced to Canton for crew training.

### March

Bathgate-Edinburgh re-opened to passengers, and Hazel Grove chord opened. Class '37' sub-Class (Nos 37310-21) created for British Steel Corporation dedicated fleet.

### April

BREL restructured into two businesses. Eight Class '20/3' created for ICI Northwich traffic.

**13** Barmouth Bridge re-opened for through traffic.

**30** Marylebone saved - official!

### May

**9** Inauguration of InterCity NW/South Coast services through Kensington Olympia.

**11** Cwmbran station opened.

**12** New 'Cambrian Coast Express' service Euston-Aberystwyth.

### June

**2** Winnersh Triangle station opened.

**10** Launch of Network SouthEast - new livery, repainted stations and new deal for passengers in London area.

**16** First sod cut on 'Thameslink' renovated Snow Hill route under Thames.

### July

APT coaches being scrapped.

**3** New Weymouth station opened.

**14** Local passenger service reintroduced on S&C - eight stations re-opened.

### August

Port-Maerdy line closed. No 144001 for testing, and '142' 'Pacers' replaced in Cornwall, due to tyre wear.

**31** RETB tested on steam (No 44767)!

### September

**1** Mickle Trafford-Dee Marsh Junction re-opened.

**8** First 'open country' masts erected on ECML in Scotland.

**28** Ystrad Rhondda and Ynyswen stations opened, but Cefn Onn closed.

### October

**2** No 89001 outshopped from Crewe.

**5** Free travel on Treherbert branch for Sports Festival.

**15** Southampton Parkway opened.

### November

**9** New world diesel speed record - Nos 43118/43109 to 144.7 mph.

**15** No 47007 named *Stratford* to celebrate trial of new depot component maintenance system.

**25** Eastbrook (Dinas Powys) and rebuilt Dorchester South stations opened.

### December

Weeks of **7th** and **14th** see standing room only as record revenues earned on Valley Lines.

**3** Prototype No 37901 named *Mirlees Pioneer*.

**8** First three '492/8' EMUs on Bournemouth semi-fasts.

## 1987

### January

'Ethels' 2 and 3 used by InterCity Charter Unit for heat on steam specials.

**11** Caersws loop closed.

**19** Ayrline electrification completed - open to Ardrossan Harbour.

### February

No 89001 tests begin from Crewe.

**15** New Trowse swing bridge opened.

**20** No 50011 *Centurion* is first of Class to be withdrawn.

### March

**1** Bramley MOD closed after BR railtour.

**11** Docklands Light Railway car 11 on special track at Gorton, to show Manchester what LRT looks like.

### April

Eight Freightliner depots closed. Class '155' DMUs unveiled - No 155301.

**1** Level 5 depots take over some Works duties.

**13** Corby-Kettering re-opened.

### May

Leeds-Manchester starts 'walk-on' concept - forget timetable

with a regular half-hour service.
**9** New Oxford-Bicester Town service.
**11** Coventry-Nuneaton re-opened to passengers after 20 years. 'Sprinters' on Trans-Pennine services - end of loco-hauled trains.

### June
Vintage DMUs back on Blaenau Ffestiniog branch, as 'Sprinters' 'screeching'!
**3** New Inverness signalling centre opened.
**27** Conwy station re-opened.

### July
Only eight of original 44 APT vehicles now intact - others cut up. Porthmadog station repainted for Eisteddfod. Meadowhall branch, Sheffield, closed.

### August
**3** New non-stop electric service Motherwell-Coatbridge.
**10** No 86432 named *Brookside* after TV soap!
**18** Last Class '27' is withdrawn.

### September
Doncaster Wagon Works privatised.
**23** No 50149 renumbered and painted in new Railfreight livery.

### October
**3** St Leonards depot closed; Thame Parkway opened.
**5** Snow Hill station, Birmingham, re-opened after 20 years.
**12** Severn Tunnel Junction marshalling complex closed.
**19** Glanrhyd bridge swept away by floods.

### November
Class '156' (No 156401) on test.
**1** Margam hump closed. New world diesel speed record - Nos 43102/43159 reach 148.5 mph.
**19** BR to sell Vale of Rheidol line.
**24** Announcement that BREL is for sale.

### December
**5** Leicester 'gap' closed and end of semaphores on Midland Main Line.
**14** First push-pull trains on WCML.
**18** First 'Wessex Electrics' ('442' 2401) handed over to BR.

### 1988

### January
No 90001 on test.

**10** Platform tickets up to 10p.
**30** New Luton-Dunstable branch laid.

### February
**9** Old Cornish clay hoods used for last time.
**12** No 91001 displayed at Crewe.
**22** North London line electrification completed.

### March
Provincial 'Express Network' launched.
**7** ECML electrification energised, Peterborough-Leeds.
**17** Annbank-Mauchline line re-opened.

### April
Anglia Region introduced.
**4** Royston-Shepreth Junction electrification.
**16** D200 withdrawn - Class now extinct on BR.
**24** New Balloch station opened.

### May
**16** Start of Thameslink services, and 'Sprinters' on Anglia-Midlands/North West.
**17** Class '60' order announced for Brush.

### June
No 141109 is first in West Yorks PTE livery.
**28** No 310073 to Wolverton Works to become No 310101 in Midline livery.
**29** End of '03s' at Ipswich.

### July
**10** Newspaper traffic lost to road.
**11** Watford-St Albans electric service starts.
**15** Shrewsbury Abbey branch closed.

### August
Decision on S&C delayed again - now five years since closure proposal! First track laid on Stansted Airport branch. No 45106 retained by InterCity Charter Train Unit and painted green.

### September
**15** No 321301 unveiled.
**22** 20,000th mast of ECML 'planted' at Durham.
**27** Aberdare branch re-opened.

### October
**3** Musselburgh station re-opened.
**10** Speedlink and Freightliners merge.

**21** Radio signalling introduced on Cambrian lines.
**31** Glanrhyd bridge re-opened.

### November
**15** Tests on longer and heavier tanker train Port Clarence-Long Eaton.
**23** Goole swing bridge hit by ship - again - threatening line.
**28** Lichfield City services extended to Trent Valley station.

### December
No 03179 new on Isle of Wight and in NSE livery.
**8** No 59004 loaned to ARC for tests against proposed Class '60' loads.
**16** Whole Class '155' fleet grounded - door problems.
**18** BR's last train on VoR.

### 1989

### January
Trowell-Radford closure proposal withdrawn.
**16** No 89001 named *Avocet* by Margaret Thatcher.
**20** East Dereham-North Elmham closed.
**22** No 47475 becomes first of Class in Provincial livery.

### February
New all-over grey general livery for Departmental locos launched.
**3** No 45106 withdrawn after fire damage.
**7** Inverness viaduct swept away by floods.
**23** No 50149 to Laira for re-conversion to original livery and identity.

### March
Seven Class '20s' to Hunslet Barclay as '20/9s' for use on weedkilling trains.
**4** Redbridge depot closed.
**17** Work starts on Channel Tunnel excavation at Shakespeare Cliff.

### April
**3** Tutbury & Hatton station opened.
**4** Network NorthWest launched.
**7** No 45128 is last 'Peak' to be withdrawn. Hednesford re-opened after 23 years.

### May
**6** End of Class '104' DMUs on Buxton services.

**12** Class '47' No 47561 repainted maroon to celebrate MCR150.
**13** Islip station opened. End of Class '33' push-pulls on Waterloo-Salisbury.

### June
**4** No 59005 arrives in UK.
**13** VoR sold to Brecon Mountain Railway.
**15** Elswick branch closed.

### July
**1** No 60001 leaves Brush for Toton.
**3** 'Stansted Express' livery launched.
**29** New Llanrwst station opened.
**30** Ironbridge Gorge station re-opened.

### August
**11** Class '321s' grounded - door problems.
**16** Class '90s' grounded - brake faults.
**25** Bugle-Carbis Wharf closed.

### September
**4** Power switched on to York on ECML.
**16** Class '59' trials in Kent, including Channel Tunnel trains.
**17** No 91010 reaches 162 mph on Stoke Bank on test.

### October
Class '313s' take over North London line. No 158701 handed over to BR.
**1** Last Class '120' DMUs withdrawn.
**9** Berry Brown station opened.

### November
**1** First waste trains in Scotland.
**8** Refurbished Deansgate station opened.
**14** Snowblower on test, Stewarts Lane-Greenford.
**25** Speedlink leaves Tyne Yard.
**27** Speedlink leaves Millerhill Yard.

### December
No 31423 (Mainline) and No 90037 (Railfreight) are first of their Classes in new liveries.
**11** No 60005 becomes first of Class in revenue-earning service.
**15** Huncoat and Cardiff Queen Street stations opened and refurbished.
**20** Last train on Chinnor branch.

# INDEX